Pra

The Gospel

Jeff and I are thankful the Lord has provided more Gospel-centered Enneagram teachers like Tyler Zach. Whether you are new to the Enneagram or have studied it for years, we know that you'll find lasting value in this book. On these pages, Tyler's creative wisdom shines, and his focus always remains on Jesus.

**—Beth & Jeff McCord, co-founders of *Your Enneagram Coach*, best-selling authors of *Becoming Us: Using the Enneagram to Create a Thriving Gospel-Centered Marriage***

What a great idea! A personalized devotional for your personality type. I love it!

**—Les Parrott, Ph.D., #1 *New York Times* bestselling author of *Saving Your Marriage Before It Starts***

[Tyler's] writing is clear, compelling, and beyond profound. In fact, I found myself struggling with underlining too much!

**—John Fooshee, president of *People Launching*, *Gospel Enneagram* founder, and Enneagram Coach trainer**

This is a must-read for any Enneagram Three desperate to know how the Achiever-mindset aligns with the gospel ... The structure of a daily devotional steeps the achievement-focused, productivity-centered, and image-obsessed in the truth of God in a loving, grace-filled, easy-to-digest way. I'll read it again and again!

**—Jill E. McCormick, writer, speaker, *Grace In Real Life* podcast host**

Piercing directly to the heart, Tyler articulates compassionately and precisely in a way that allows the gift of hope type 3s already possess to be illuminated to the world. A must-read for any Type 3 or people in close relationship with one.

**—Meredith W. Boggs, blogger, *The Other Half* podcast host**

When you spend 40 days journeying through these pages, you'll surely find insights into how our "threeness" trips us up. You'll also be reminded to journey back home to the God who invites us to a more fulfilling life than any achievement can provide.

**—Dr. Drew Moser, author of *The Enneagram of Discernment: The Way of Vocation, Wisdom, and Practice*; co-host, *Fathoms | An Enneagram Podcast***

Brilliantly relevant and immensely empowering, this book is one I want all my Enneagram 3 friends to read.

**—Twyla Franz, writer, *The Uncommon Normal* podcast host**

I'm glad to see Tyler Zach's new book on the gospel and the Enneagram, especially its devotional format oriented specifically for Type 3.

**—Dr. Gregg Allison, professor of Christian Theology at The Southern Baptist Theological Seminary, elder at Sojourn Community Church, author of *50 Core Truths of the Christian Faith*, *Historical Theology*, *The Holy Spirit*, and more**

Wow, the way Tyler helps Type Threes understand that their gifts and desires are not something to be ashamed of really hit home for me. As a fellow three, it's easy to feel ashamed for wanting to be successful. What Tyler helps us all remember is the importance of where our heart is and how it needs to be aligned with Christ ... This is an incredible book ...

**—Callie Ammons, *Living Enneagram* podcast host**

As an Enneagram 3 myself, I felt seen and understood, as well as challenged. This is a book that I will come back to again and again to reaffirm the truth about how God has made me, and how to live in that truth consistently.

**—Gina Butz, director of Leadership Evaluation and Formation, Cru Global Team; author of *Making Peace with Change: Navigating Life's Messy Transitions with Honesty and Grace***

As an Enneagram coach, it can be difficult to find devotional materials to recommend that speak directly to the Type-specific strengths and struggles while keeping Biblical truth and grace as the focus. *The Gospel for Achievers* is the perfect pairing of these two ideas, and I believe every Enneagram Three would benefit from Tyler's encouraging words.

**—Kim Eddy, Christian Enneagram coach**

# The Gospel for Achievers

A 40-Day Devotional for Driven, Successful Go-Getters

BY TYLER ZACH

Edited by Joshua Casey and Stephanie Cross

*The Gospel For Achievers: A 40-Day Devotional for Driven, Successful Go-Getters (Enneagram 3)*



Edited by Joshua Casey and Stephanie Cross


To request permission, contact the author at *tyler@gospelforenneagram.com*.



*Cover and Interior Design:*
*Fruitful Design* (www.fruitful.design)

ISBN: 9798643530381

www.gospelforenneagram.com

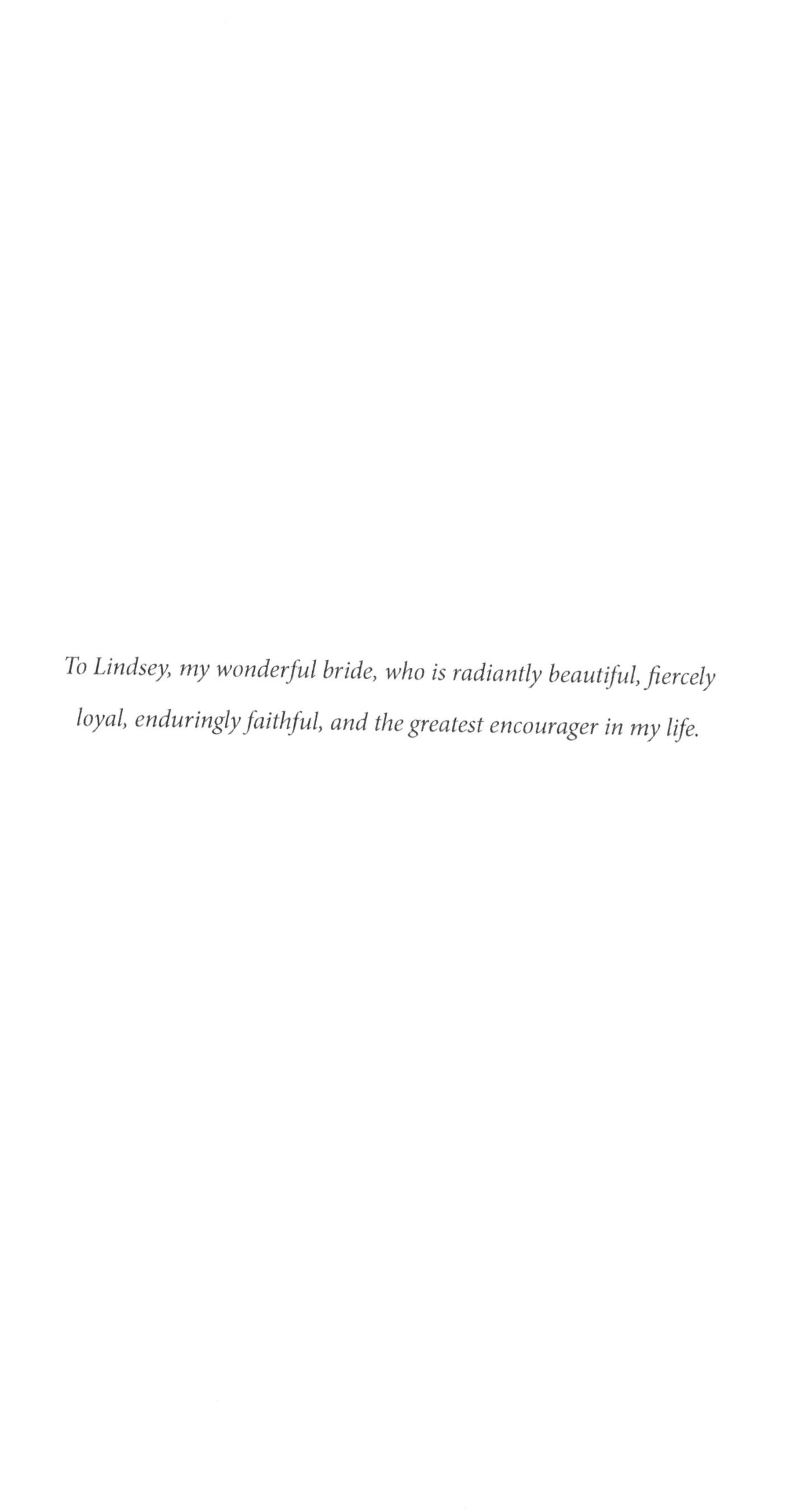

*To Lindsey, my wonderful bride, who is radiantly beautiful, fiercely loyal, enduringly faithful, and the greatest encourager in my life.*

# *Table of Contents*

# *Foreword*

When Jeff and I first discovered the Enneagram, it wasn't easy finding books written from a Christian worldview. We understood how important Gospel-centered Enneagram resources could be, and that inspired us to start our business, *Your Enneagram Coach*. Since then, we've helped over 1,000,000 people find their Type through our free assessment, and grow through our online classes, coaching certifications, books, and now a podcast.

While Jeff is a Type 6 and I am a Type 9, we connect with Type 3 through the lines (Enneagram Paths) in the Enneagram symbol, which means we can take on Type 3 characteristics depending on our circumstances. When Jeff and I use the healthy aspects of Type 3, it leads us to greater efficiency, optimism, and a drivenness to succeed. We are thankful for these gifts. We would not be where we are today without accessing the amazing qualities the Type 3 offers.

The Enneagram is a tool that clarifies our fallen nature while also reminding us we are created in the Imago Dei (image of God). When Jeff and I understood the *why* behind our thoughts and actions, it transformed how we looked at ourselves, our relationship with God, our marriage, our parenting, and (obviously) our careers. Taking a risk by starting a business was both exciting and terrifying. We could have easily spun out of control or run out of gas (at times we did!), but knowing the Enneagram, as seen through the lens of the Gospel, kept us grounded and on track.

The world needs Type 3s. When you set your mind to something, you deliver. Your established networks connect people and open doors to new opportunities. Your charisma and self-confidence inspire others to reach their goals, and you're always behind them, cheering and coaching them on!

Like all numbers, Type 3s can have seasons of struggle. It can be difficult for you to find rest and just BE. The Enneagram can help you recognize when your unhealthy ambitions are controlling you. You can stop, rest, and refocus on Jesus and what He wants you to do (or not do!). Type 3s, we are confident this 40-day devotional will guide you toward a more balanced YOU.

Jeff and I are thankful the Lord has provided more Gospel-centered Enneagram teachers like Tyler Zach. Whether you are new to the Enneagram or have studied it for years, we know that you'll find lasting value in this book. On these pages, Tyler's creative wisdom shines, and his focus always remains on Jesus. We're praying that God will meet you on these pages, and you will recognize your inherent value as His beloved child.

Jesus is the author and perfecter of our faith (Hebrews 12:2). He finished the great task He set out to do (John 19:30). A vital part of His ministry was to stay in alignment with His Father, and He did this by setting aside time for rest and reflection. He invites you to do the same, to come away, to separate from the crowds, and BE with Him. Remember, you are loved and valued for simply being you. You do not have to win Christ's approval. You are accepted right now as you are.

**—Beth and Jeff McCord**
co-founders of *Your Enneagram Coach*
best-selling authors of *Becoming Us: Using the Enneagram to Create a Thriving Gospel-Centered Marriage*

# *Introduction:*
# The Gospel for Achievers

*I'm proud of you.* You slowed down enough to read this book! That's no easy task for an Achiever, but let me tell you, it'll be productive in the long run.

As an Achiever myself, I am tempted to believe living life is like treading water—if I stop accomplishing, I'll sink. My greatest fear has always been standing before God at the end of my life and hearing Him say, "You didn't do enough." But I've come to realize the voice I hear is *mine*, not His. Ultimately, this book is all about slowing down enough to hear God's affirming voice—the One who loves you into your full self and defines what true success looks like.

His "scorecard" is vastly different from the ones we keep, mostly because there is no scorecard with God. Contrary to the belief that what God wants most for us is to get more stuff done, His primary goal is to be with us and transform us into the image of His Son. On this journey, you'll learn what it looks like to be a human being, not a human doing. You'll find out how to embrace your emotions as natural and even helpful. And you'll become more honest and authentic, taking off the mask and finding your identity in God rather than what you do or with whom you are associated.

There is no fast-track to spiritual growth, which is what we'd all prefer. But here's the good news: as you create space over the next 40 days to reflect on the gospel more and slow down to do less, you'll come to the wonderful (and scary) realization that the world will keep spinning while you rest. God is on the throne. Don't worry; He's got it! You are an integral part of this beautiful creation God continues to sustain—if you weren't here, it would be incomplete. But, while God wants to use you in the ongoing unfolding of His plan to reconcile all things to Himself, He won't force you.

He wired you to accomplish a lot of quality things quickly, but ultimately created the world to be dependent on *Him*, not you. Your first job—before doing anything—is to *be*, to rest in His sufficiency for you. Because He is on the throne, you can feel the freedom to slow down and let God reorient your life around His definition of success.

Because self-awareness is a necessary part of spiritual growth, the Enneagram can be helpful. Unlike other "personality" profiles such as *Clifton StrengthsFinder®* and *Myers-Briggs Type Indicator®*, the aim of the Enneagram is to uncover why we do what we do—to help us see what lies behind our strengths and weaknesses. If we use it as a diagnostic tool and allow the Bible to provide the language for our interpretation, it can produce great change in our lives, relationships, and work.

This is a book about our Enneagram type but don't be mistaken. Fundamentally, I'm a church planter and pastor who believes the Bible is the inspired Word of God and is sufficient for all He requires us to believe and do. But I also believe God has provided additional insights in fields such as medicine and psychology that are helpful in understanding the incredible world God has made. For instance, my wife, Lindsey, and I have really learned a lot from experts in these fields as we have sought to be the best parents for our youngest son, Zeke, who is on the autism spectrum.

I admit, we must tread carefully as we draw insights from fields with limited horizons of evidence like psychology (we still have so much more to learn about the brain!). But as with anything we come across in this fallible world, we can put on our gospel lens and make use of what God has provided to us through His common grace.

### What Makes This Book Different?

While there are other projects explaining the Enneagram, the primary aim of this book is to go deeper by applying the truth of God's Word specifically to your type over the next 40 days. If you are suspicious of the Enneagram or know someone who is, download my free resource called "Should Christians Use The Enneagram?" at gospelforenneagram.com. I pray that it will help you engage with the Enneagram as a Christian and talk about it with others.

Before we get to the daily devotions, let's look at how the gospel both affirms and challenges the unique characteristics of your type.

### The Gospel Affirms Achievers

God sympathizes with the worldview of an Achiever. This chaotic world truly does lack order, is slowed down by unnecessary setbacks, and needs leaders who will organize the chaos, make plans, and get results. Therefore, an Achiever will be happy to know that the Bible affirms the following beliefs:

- **God created us to be productive.** "And God blessed them. And God said to them, 'Be fruitful and multiply and fill the earth and subdue it, and have dominion over the fish of the sea and over the birds of the heavens and over every living thing that moves on the earth.'"[1]

- **God created us to be faithful stewards.** "His master said to him, 'Well done, good and faithful servant. You have been faithful over a little; I will set you over much. Enter into the joy of your master.'"[2]

- **God created us to be efficient.** "Look carefully then how you walk, not as unwise but as wise, making the best use of the time, because the days are evil. Therefore do not be foolish, but understand what the will of the Lord is."[3]

- **God created us to work hard.** "Go to the ant, O sluggard; consider her ways, and be wise. Without having any chief, officer, or ruler, she prepares her bread in summer and gathers her food in harvest."[4]

- **God created us to give others hope.** "May the God of hope fill you with all joy and peace in believing, so that by the power of the Holy Spirit you may abound in hope."[5]

### The Gospel Challenges Achievers

The gospel also provides specific challenges to Achievers. Now we'll explore the most common lies Achievers believe and watch how the Bible provides much better promises and blessings.

---

1 Gen. 1:28 English Standard Version.

2 Matt. 25:23

3 Eph. 5:15-17

4 Prov. 6:6-8

5 Rom. 15:13

- **Lie #1: Image is everything.** Achievers want everyone to see their ideal image: someone who is cool, calm, effective, competent, and never idle. Unfortunately, this means we think an awful lot about our image during the day. Thus, while the mental fixation of an achiever is vanity, the truth is that God's glory should be our greatest aim.

- **Lie #2: I am loved for what I do.** The deepest longing of an Achiever is to be loved for who you are, not what you do. Christ Jesus is the one who can convey that deep sense of being loved—you are fully accepted not on the basis of *your* failures or successes, but *His*.

- **Lie #3: I must avoid failure at all costs.** If appearing successful is the primary goal of the Achiever, then failure will be avoided at all costs. But the truth is that failure is not fatal for the Christian, because the fear of failure has been erased by Jesus's justification, meaning Christ has taken our failures and exchanged them for His successes.

- **Lie #4: I'm only as good as my last success.** When your self-esteem is deflated by a failure or your public persona begins to lose popularity, you'll be tempted to use a defense mechanism called *identification*. This means you'll search for whatever image is successful in others' eyes and adopt that as your own. But the truth is that your identity is secure in Christ.

- **Lie #5: I must wear a mask to be accepted.** This lie will tell you to appear confident and successful at all times; that you must hide the parts of yourself you think aren't as impressive to others. But hiding in shame will keep you perpetually trapped into thinking you are only loved for appearing successful. The truth is that Jesus died on the cross for your *flawed* self, not your accomplished self. When you believe this, it will transform the vice of deceit into the virtue of truthfulness.

- **Lie #6: I must go faster to get ahead.** When the good desire for efficiency becomes ultimate, there will be a temptation to "be like God" in His ability and capacity. This will cause you to act like a human *doing*. You'll create a relational separation between yourself and others, be tempted to take shortcuts on integrity, and prioritize public performance over private devotions. Ultimately, this will lead to burnout and despair. The truth is that you must slow down to love God and others because love always trumps productivity.

As you can see, the gospel will challenge your perception of who the protagonists and antagonists are in your life. In an Achiever's kingdom, those who look the best and are the most productive are rewarded. Your "heroes" become those who boost your self-esteem, make you look good, and support your work habits. Likewise, your "villains" will become those who slow down your progress through laziness, pessimism, heavy emotions, warnings, negative feedback, or interruptions.

However, God's kingdom will not be filled with those who climbed the success ladder faster, but rather with those who cast the crown of their successes at the feet of Jesus. In this place, there is no pretending or performing allowed. In this place substance eats style for breakfast. In this place, things like interruptions, feelings, failures, and other perceived obstacles are really not obstacles, but God's means of grace used to bring about spiritual growth.

### The Invitation

When Jesus Christ, the Divine All in All, entered into flawed and limited human history, He started His mission with an invitation: "The time is fulfilled, and the kingdom of God is at hand; repent and believe in the gospel."[6] He explained that to enter the good life, the sort of eternally renewing life that begins well before the grave, you must do two things: believe the truth and turn from sin. Believing includes acknowledging who God is, who He says we are, and what He has done for us; turning includes shedding our false worldview, misplaced desires, defense mechanisms, strategies we use to run and hide from God, and self-salvation efforts.

If you are ready to begin this incredible 40-day journey and accept God's invitation, then let's go! It's going to be an enlightening ride. I suspect you will grow rapidly in the days to come as you become more self-aware and experience newfound freedom. I believe you will encounter many "aha" moments as you read profound truths for your type. I guarantee the things you learn about yourself in this book will stick with you the rest of your life.

---

6 Mark 1:15

# Day 1:

# Image is Everything

*"So God created man in his own image, in the image of God he created him; male and female he created them."*

—Genesis 1:27

MOST PEOPLE CLAIM NOT TO CARE ABOUT their image. Some say this to appear confident, while some believe caring too much about how others perceive them is shallow—like a celebrity focused on their "brand." But normal folks aren't supposed to care because, as the adage goes: When you're young, you care what people think about you. When you grow up, you try not to care what people think about you. When you get old, you realize they weren't thinking about you at all.

> Image is everything.
>
> –Andre Agassi[1]

Yet when we're honest, most of us can admit we really do care. And it's actually okay to feel that way; it's in our make-up to care about image. Humans initially lived as a tribal species to navigate a dangerous world. Mirroring each other helps us stay safe, get along, and get ahead in life. But more importantly, God created us as "mirrors," reflecting

1 Ian Morgan Cron and Suzanne Stabile, *The Road Back to You*, Kindle edition (Ivp Books, 2016), 135.

His heart and character to a broken and hurting world. We are truly the Imago Dei, translating the infinite, invisible One for a finite, visible world.

But this mirror was cracked from top to bottom when we "exchanged the glory of God for the glory of man."[2] And it's not even a mistake relegated to people of the past; it's something we all do. In other words, it's not just what happened; it's what happens. Though it looks different for each person and personality type, we all do it all the time. In Enneagram-speak, most Achievers express this exchange of God's glory by focusing on the person in the mirror. Rather than expressing the image of God, we try to express our own ideal image. As Pastor Garrett Kell says, "The desire for God to be glorified through me is the height of my created purpose. But there is a fine line between wanting God to use you for his glory and wanting everyone to know it."[3]

> Jesus died on the cross for your flawed self, not your successful self.

Even when you are trying to do "great things for God," you may still find a way to "photobomb" Jesus. And if we're honest, we usually know when we're doing it. It's not hard to find a clever way to jump into everyone's field of view and take the credit Jesus alone deserves. When we're making a positive impact in this world, it's not because our tailored image is front and center, but because the Imago Dei is shining through.

It is difficult to accept that Someone we can neither see nor touch is our ultimate source of acceptance, so we drift from the gospel's promise of unconditional love and work hard to project a favorable image to those we can see and touch. We become master sculptors, crafting an image. We pick up the chisel and begin carving the perfect persona for others to admire, handing over our God-given need for acceptance to people rather than God—"exchanging the glory of God for the glory of man."

But it'll never be enough.

---

2 Rom. 1:23

3 Garrett Kell, "Stop Photobombing Jesus," The Gospel Coalition, 2017, https://www.thegospelcoalition.org/article/stop-photobombing-jesus/.

***The Good News for Achievers*** is Jesus died on the cross for you—for your flawed self, not your successful, accomplished, crafted self. You can put the chisel down because you are His workmanship. You are, right now without any effort, the Imago Dei. The Holy Spirit is working like a master sculptor to clear away the excess marble and reveal what God sees underneath the image you work so hard to present to others. The Creator and Sustainer of all loves you still, because when He looks in your mirror, He sees the imago of His Son and says, "with you I am well pleased."[4]

### → Pray

Father, forgive me for looking in the mirror too much. I've served my image, not Yours. I spend so much of my day fixated on how others see me rather than how You see me. Cleanse my heart of every inclination to steal the glory You deserve so I can exchange it for human admiration. Remind me that Your Son's death is proof I don't need to pursue any other acceptance than Yours, which You already gave. Amen.

4 Mark 1:11

# Day 1 Reflections

**What aspects of your own image do you spend the most time sculpting?**

**Why do you think Jesus was not concerned with maintaining a good image?**

**How would your life change if you stopped seeking others' approval?**

## → Respond

Write out all the reasons God loves you without listing any of your titles, roles, or accomplishments.

## *Day 2:*

# Wearing a Million Masks

*But when I saw that their conduct was not in step with the truth of the gospel, I said to Cephas before them all, "If you, though a Jew, live like a Gentile and not like a Jew, how can you force the Gentiles to live like Jews?"*

—Galatians 2:14

---

ONE OF THE ACHIEVER'S "SUPERPOWERS" IS THE ability to observe what others are feeling and become who they need you to be. That's why many become, in large and small ways, leaders and public figures. They are the celebrities, the politicians and pastors, the homecoming kings and queens, class presidents, and employees of the year.

> I like changing personalities.
>
> —Mick Jagger

Achievers are master compartmentalizers and natural chameleons, always adapting and shape-shifting to meet the expectations of the people around them. They can belong to different groups with different lifestyles, changing their role with lightning speed as they go from one room to another. Like a Broadway actor between scenes, there is no end to the amount of costumes and masks an Achiever can wear.[1] In Ian Cron and Suzanne Stabile's *The Road Back To You*, a story was shared of one pastor who half-jokingly said, "[Achievers] don't have one persona, we are Legion."[2]

The danger of wearing multiple masks comes when we are forced to interact with two people or groups we have tried to keep separate. In his letter to the Galatians, the Apostle Paul recalls a time he called out Peter on this very issue. While in Antioch, Peter gave the Gentiles the impression he was comfortable eating with them (a sign of acceptance). However, when the more orthodox Jewish-Christian leaders showed up from Jerusalem, Peter distanced himself from the new Gentile converts, creating a rift in the fledgling community. Paul, who had worked so hard to bring these groups together, called out this duplicitous behavior, reminding Peter that such hypocrisy was out of step with the gospel.

> You were not created to be a prisoner to the expectations of others.

Peter's experience is one of our worst fears coming true. Imagine having all the people you know from different circles of relationships (e.g. family, co-workers, church friends, etc.) showing up in your living room at the same time. We may be able to switch between two personas quickly, but we can't be both at the same time!

Are you exhausted from trying to be who others want you to be? This unhealthy side of the Achiever is a tiring role to play. As artist Ryan O'Neal from Sleeping At Last sings, "It's so exhausting on this silver screen where I play the role of anyone but me."[3]

***The Good News for Achievers*** is that God created you to be your redeemed self and no one else. You were not created to be a prisoner to the expectations of others. Keeping the mask on indefinitely will only perpetuate the lie that you are not loved for who you really are, but for what you do. You are the one Christ lived and died for, and with Him we never have to be someone else.

---

1 Richard Rohr and Andreas Ebert, *The Enneagram: A Christian Perspective*, Kindle edition (Crossroad, 2001), 83.

2 Cron and Stabile, *The Road*, 134.

3 Ryan Neal, "Sleeping At Last," Sleeping At Last, 2016, http://sleepingatlast.com.

### → Pray

Father, You created me perfect in Your image. Forgive me for the masks I wear to conform not to Your will, but the wills of others. Thank You for sending Jesus to die for the imperfect person behind the mask so that I might die to the expectations of others and be my redeemed self. Amen.

# Day 2 Reflections

**How has your ability to adapt to different groups and situations allowed you to make a positive impact?**

**In what situations do you find yourself in "acting mode," suppressing your true emotions to maintain what you believe to be the "right" image for that situation?**

**How do the masks you wear hinder your personal well-being and intimacy with God and others?**

**Have you ever spent time with someone who was completely authentic? What was it like knowing without a doubt that you were interacting with their real self?**

## → Respond

Create two columns on this page or in a journal. In one column, write down how you see yourself. In another column, write down how you think others see you. Under your list, write down one action step you can take to reveal your authentic self more to others and to merge those columns together.

*Day 3:*

# The Spell of Shame

*So when the woman saw that the tree was good for food, and that it was a delight to the eyes, and that the tree was to be desired to make one wise, she took of its fruit and ate, and she also gave some to her husband who was with her, and he ate. Then the eyes of both were opened, and they knew that they were naked. And they sewed fig leaves together and made themselves loincloths.*

—Genesis 3:6-7

---

SHAME IS AN EMOTION ACHIEVERS ARE ALMOST always feeling but never let anyone see. While some personalities cannot hide their shame, Achievers have the ability to appear self-confident in all situations—not because they know they're awesome but because they're hoping someone will tell them they are. But in the absence of this constant approval, what will cover the nagging sense of lack?

> I finally see myself. Unabridged and overwhelmed, a mess of a story I'm ashamed to tell, but I'm slowly learning how to break this spell.
>
> —Sleeping At Last, "Three"

We all have an Accuser within us, an Enemy who shows up whenever we fail to bring condemnation through others' voices or even our own. Someone who steps in to tell us we are irreparable; that our separation from the One who loves us is an impossible chasm to cross. This Accuser[1] dwells within each of us, biding his time until distractions fall away and we are vulnerable to his lies. As tennis great Andre Agassi shared, "I've been cheered by thousands, booed by thousands, but nothing feels as bad as the booing inside your own head during those ten minutes before you fall asleep."[2]

What do you do when shame creeps in? When the distractions and feelings of accomplishment fade and you're left alone with your Accuser? After eating the forbidden fruit, Adam and Eve sewed fig leaves to cover the awful feeling of being naked and exposed. It's an unpleasant feeling for everyone, but particularly unbearable for Achievers. Remember, image and others' perceptions are everything. We would do almost anything to cover up the gap between the truth and what they (and we) expect us to be like.

> Shame is powerless to actually effect change within ourselves or others.

There are numerous ways Achievers conceal shame. We often ignore or downplay mistakes, even reframing them as successes. We can justify them by our good intentions or cultivate an ongoing defensive posture, which is quite effective at repelling people from ever offering feedback.[3] But none of these concealments ever actually get rid of the shame that follows us everywhere we go, no matter what fig leaves we try putting between ourselves and the feeling.

Unlike guilt, which can have positive effects if it leads to life change, shame is an entirely negative emotion that only exists to convince us of our deficiencies. It is powerless to actually effect change within ourselves or others. Guilt can lead to confession and restoration, but shame leads only to concealment.

---

1 In rabbinical thought, *ha-Sâtan* ("the Satan," translated as "The Accuser") was a member of the court of heaven who stood before God's throne, condemning His people. As he did with Job, Satan would try to convince God that His children were lying to Him, that they were in fact not worthy of love. The rabbis took this a step further, claiming this Accuser dwelt within each of us, not as a particular being, but as that part of our hearts always telling us we are not worthy of love and acceptance.

2 Andre Agassi, *Open: An Autobiography* (Knopf Doubleday, 2009), 272.

3 Robert H Thune, T*he Gospel-Centered Life: Study Guide with Leader's Notes* (New Growth Press, 2018).

How do we break the spell?

When Adam and Eve were naked in shame, God mercifully pursues them and replaces their fragile fig leaves with better garments. They are completely unable to break the spell of shame on their own or even come to God for help in their failure. But God comes to them, making the necessary sacrifice to cover them in His mercy, just as the prodigal son is met by his father on the road and covered by his father's grace and mercy.

***The Good News for Achievers*** is that we are not alone. Jesus knows the creeping voice of the Accuser. Our innocent Savior took our place on the cross and was publicly humiliated. The cross was intended to shame Him, but Jesus turned the narrative on its head. He despised the cross's shame and, in the process, made a spectacle of the Accuser's powerlessness in the light of God's love and mercy. The spell is broken and the voice of shame has been defeated.

**→ Pray**

Father, there is a lot that I am ashamed about, but I praise You today for drawing near to me when I feel unworthy. You sent Jesus to defeat shame and free me from it. By the power of the Holy Spirit, help me to no longer feel the need to hide myself from You or others, and help me to be true to who You've made me to be. Amen.

# Day 3 Reflections

**When are you the most likely to feel ashamed?**

**What is your "go-to" defense mechanism for deflecting shame?**

**How would practicing the ongoing habit of confessing your sin to others break the spell of shame in your life?**

## → Respond

Today, reveal something you may feel ashamed of to a safe person who can speak God's grace over you.

## *Day 4:*

# People Are the Task

*But Martha was distracted with much serving. And she went up to him and said, "Lord, do you not care that my sister has left me to serve alone? Tell her then to help me."*

—Luke 10:40

---

MAKE NO MISTAKE: THE WORLD NEEDS "TASKERS." Families, companies, and churches need women and men who have checklists, plans, goals, and solutions; people who can stay focused and get things done quickly and with quality.

> Loving people the way Jesus did is great theology.
>
> –Bob Goff

However, a problem arises when tasks are prioritized over people. Ian Cron points out that Achievers are often addicted to viewing life as a series of tasks to be completed, an approach that can then be turned onto those they love:

> [Threes] can unconsciously view their partner or their relationship with them like an action item on their task-management list. Those people can become one of the many projects they're working on at any given time. For instance, you might hear Threes talk about how they and their

> partner sit down once a year to set spiritual, financial, physical or social goals for their marriage or relationship or to discuss ways in which they can make the day-to-day management of the family more efficient or productive. Clearly being intentional about relationships is admirable, so long as they remain spiritual unions we cultivate, not business partnerships we manage.[1]

How do you view or treat people when your Type A, tasker mode kicks into full gear? Do you really listen and receive input from others as you work toward a goal?[2] Have you found yourself intentionally avoiding high-maintenance people, those who aren't easily intimidated by your management, or those whose gifts and opinions you don't esteem as highly? Marilyn Vancil insightfully adds that Achievers "genuinely care about people and enjoy many relationships but don't often set aside time or energy to invest in those who aren't in their immediate scope of action."[3]

> A problem arises when tasks are prioritized over people.

Do you get so focused on your tasks that you forget people are the point? That the tasks we create are there to help us build meaningful "spiritual unions" rather than business partnerships? Too often, Achievers can use others to accomplish their lofty goals, leaving hurt and ignored people in their wake—people who feel like they were merely a box for the Achiever to check. A clean house, a new business venture, a successful book, brand, or event may be impressive and can do good in the world, but they aren't the point: relationships are.

Martha, distracted with her tasks, is more concerned about impressing Jesus than being with Him. But Jesus looks at her soul and sees someone "anxious" about her to-do list—someone who thought the way to the Divine heart was to impress Him with her titanic accomplishments in the face of adversity. So He interjects to say that her sister, Mary, has accomplished the most important task of the day—sitting at His feet. Did Martha ever get it? Was she able to move beyond her hurt

---

1 Cron and Stabile, *The Road*, 140.

2 Beatrice Chestnut, *The 9 Types of Leadership: Mastering the Art of People in the 21st Century Workplace*, Kindle edition (Post Hill Press, 2017), 112.

3 Marilyn Vancil, *Self to Lose Self to Find: Using the Enneagram to Uncover Your True, God-gifted Self*, (New York: Convergent, 2020), 82.

feelings and learn to move slowly through a crowd, as her Lord did? Did she ever learn to choose what was truly necessary?

***The Good News for Achievers*** is that Jesus never graded His followers on their accomplishments but on the *way they pursued them*. We can drop the striving and learn to stop and sit at our Maker's feet. We don't have to figure this out on our own. Over and over again, Jesus focused on the how rather than the what, giving us a perfect example for how we ourselves can learn to lead. All we have to do is stop and remember that God prioritizes us every day, not because we are useful, but because we are valuable. And He asks us to see others in the same way.

## → Pray

Father, thank You for being a relational God who pursues me every day. I was created to know You deeply but am distracted by many things. Help me to sit at the feet of Jesus today and enjoy Your transforming presence. Holy Spirit, loosen my grip on my tasks and give me a greater love, especially for those the world misses because Jesus, the truest success, was a man despised and rejected by the world. Help me to see and hear Him in the meek and lowly. Amen.

# Day 4 Reflections

**Who or what is getting sacrificed right now for your tasks (marriage, kids, staff team, health, etc.)?**

**Why is it so hard to want to be around people who are poor, struggling, or on the bottom of the totem pole? Why did Jesus not seem to find it hard to prioritize them?**

**How can I make more room for casual conversation during the day that doesn't revolve around work but strengthens relationships?**

## → Respond

Plan 25 percent less work this week than you normally do to allow for more relational time. As you do less, ask others how you can serve or support their work.

## *Day 5:*

# Less Obvious Narcissism

*So all the people took off the rings of gold that were in their ears and brought them to Aaron. And he received the gold from their hand and fashioned it with a graving tool and made a golden calf. And they said, "These are your gods, O Israel, who brought you up out of the land of Egypt!"*

—Exodus 32:3-4

---

HAVE YOU EVER BEEN ACCUSED OF BEING narcissistic, proud, or arrogant? Though Achievers rarely get described in such ways (at least in public), the concept of vainglory, or excessive vanity, is often described as an unhealthy area for this personality.

> Man's chief end is to glorify God and enjoy him forever.
>
> —Westminster Shorter Catechism

One of my favorite Enneagram books, Marilyn Vancil's *Self to Lose Self to Find*, describes vainglory as the Achiever's fixation on their external persona rather than their internal world.[1] This means that when the Achiever isn't mindful, they spend a disproportionate amount of time and energy on managing others' impressions.

1 Vancil, M, *Self to Lose*, 83.

Molding the masks, chiseling away at the sculpture, so it can match exactly the changeable desires of the people surrounding us. You can see the danger here: when left unchecked, this process can go on until there is nothing left of you.

Aaron, Moses' brother, did not appear to suffer from excessive vanity. But when Moses goes up the mountain and the Israelites get restless, they come to his brother and he molds himself to fit their expectations, giving them the golden calf they want. Whether he is afraid of the mob, trying to make a play for Moses's role, or legitimately worried for his fearful people, he gives in to please the crowd.

This isn't be the only time the charismatic leader will (potentially) attempt to steal the spotlight from his brother in order to increase his stature.[2] Although he spends a great deal of time and energy laboring on the golden calf, he is at the same time crafting a golden image of himself to impress the people. Maybe he is just trying to help them, but if he can look good while doing it—well that is just making the most of the situation.

> The Achiever spends a disproportionate amount of time and energy on managing others' impressions.

Though you may not be drawing attention to yourself so obviously, what are you working on that could lead to "photobombing" Jesus, increasing your stature and feeding the narcissistic need for glory? (Which, again, is simply the need to get approval from anywhere other than God.)

Thinking about ourselves too much will eventually take its toll on relationships and reduce our ability to show empathy, like the Pharisee in the Gospel of Luke whose prayer is so out of touch with God's desires for us that he begins with, "God, I thank you that I am not like…"[3]

As inner-narcissism grows, Achievers begin to create one-way relationships because, as Riso and Hudson explain, "Both parties are in love with the same person: the [Achiever]."[4] This ultimately dehumanizes others and turns them

---

2 cf. Numbers 12

3 Luke 18:9-17

4 Don Richard Riso and Russ Hudson, *The Wisdom of the Enneagram : The Complete Guide to Psychological and Spiritual Growth for the Nine Personality Types*, Kindle edition (New York: Bantam Books, 1999), 100.

into "narcissistic suppliers." When narcissism is full-blown, it means Achievers "cannot live with people and they cannot live without them, because they are hostile toward the people on whom they depend, and because they feel like 'nobody' without the attention of others."[5]

How does Moses respond to his narcissistic brother when he gets back down the mountain?[6] He takes Aaron's golden image, burns it with fire, and grinds it up into powder. What's more, he makes the people drink the contaminated waters as a reminder of the bitterness of putting faith in such things. How often do we lead our people to the bitter waters of our narcissism simply because we can't let our image and need for approval go?

***The Good News for Achievers*** is that Jesus has shown us the way into this path of downward mobility out of narcissism. As Paul sings in his letter to the Philippians, Jesus shows us the true nature of humanity by "making himself a servant—being made in human likeness."[7] He allowed any vainglory within Himself to die so that He could be raised in humility to God and bring us along with Him. Though we have taken all of the jewelry of our successes and melted them into a golden image of ourselves, we must now grind it up into powder. We must, "count everything as loss" compared to the surpassing value of knowing Jesus, the One who has gone before to show us the way into loving, humble service.

## → Pray

Father, You are the Lord and You will not give Your glory to another. Like Aaron, who sabotaged Your work through Moses, I too am in danger of sabotaging the ministry You've give me by making it all about me. Forgive me for thinking about myself too often, for focusing on the me I see in the mirror instead of Your image reflected from within. Fill me with the Holy Spirit to join Him in the work of glorifying Your Son, Jesus.

---

5 Riso and Hudson, *The Wisdom*, 101.

6 (Other than throwing a fit and breaking the stone tablets.)

7 Philippians 2:7

# Day 5 Reflections

**What is your "golden calf?" What have you been working on that you are hoping will draw attention to yourself?**

**How much of the day do you think about yourself? What can you do today to get the attention off of you and onto Jesus? What are some practices that could center you on Christ?**

**What activities heighten your pleasure in God? How can you do them more?**

## → Respond

Do something today that stirs your delight and pleasure in God (listen to music, take a prayer walk, listen to a sermon, go on a retreat, hike, etc.).

## *Day 6:*

# Failure Isn't Fatal

*For the righteous falls seven times and rises again, but the wicked stumble in times of calamity.*

—Proverbs 24:16

---

THERE IS A WORD MANY ACHIEVERS HAVE struck from their vocabularies: failure.

As Beatrice Chestnut explains,

> [Achievers] like to move fast, and can get bored or impatient if they can't move on to the next thing. They avoid failure, can smell it a mile away and will change course if necessary to make sure it doesn't happen.[1]

> If the foundation is right, you can always rebuild.
>
> –Myron Pierce

But failure does not have to be fatal—it can become a formative force in life. It doesn't have to be the "end of you," but the means to a better end. Rather than a detour, it is the very path to success, revealing the house of straw we might have built with untested,

1 Chestnut, *9 Types*, 112.

faulty beliefs and practices that won't offer protection in difficult seasons. Failure can be a gift, revealing the mistakes and traps keeping us from moving forward.

Aside from recognizing failure as a useful teacher, we must accept it because it is inevitable. Almost every hero in Scripture failed miserably. Look no further than Moses—the great prophet and bringer of the law—who, in a fit of anger strikes the rock, publicly dishonoring the command of God. Look to Peter—the rock—who denies even knowing Jesus when things get tough. Look to the Apostle Paul who spends his early years zealously killing Christians. Look to David—the "man after God's own heart"—who commits adultery, deception, and murder.

But none of these failures, abysmal as they were, ended up being the end of these people's stories. All of their stories include opportunities for recognizing mistakes, seeking forgiveness, and moving forward as wiser people. Moses learns compassion for his people. David is confronted by the prophet Nathan and pours out his soul in Psalm 51, asking for a clean heart—giving generations of God-followers words of contrition and forgiveness. Peter and Paul both move forward as humbler and wiser servants, able to offer grace and forgiveness to others after having received it themselves. These fresh starts don't negate the consequences of their actions, but each "hero" is still able to change and continue following their path of service for God.

> Failure does not have to be fatal, but a formative force in life.

Failure will feel like a fatal blow when our identity is wrapped up in performance. Our work and achievements are like limbs—they become part of us and we feel attacked when our beloved projects are critiqued and questioned or simply don't pan out. But when we find our identity in Christ, we can humbly allow His success to cover our faults and failures and be reminded that nothing has or can separate us from God's loving acceptance.

***The Good News for Achievers*** is that failure can become something different, changing from an attack on our identity into part of the process of sanctification. Rather than reframing failure to save face, we can add the word into our vocabulary, making us more honest and transparent people. Richard Rohr insightfully points out that the cross will always be a "symbol of failure" to the world.[2] Our culture avoids failure at all costs, but we have been called to take up our cross, remembering that our greatest success came through one Man's apparent failure.

### → Pray

Father, I am more flawed than I ever imagined, but You are more loving than I ever dared hope. Accept me into Your loving arms just as the father did with his prodigal son. Graciously remind me that there is no failure that is too big for the cross. Help me to be honest about my shortcomings and to extend to others the same mercy You've given to me.

2 Rohr and Ebert, *The Enneagram,* 84.

# Day 6 Reflections

**How have you reframed past failures as partial successes?**

**How does the gospel free you to be a less defensive person?**

**How will embracing failure as a part of life help you be more accepting of yourself and others?**

## → Respond

Be bold enough to share one of your past failures with someone today.

## *Day 7:*

# Gettin' Stuff Done

*And God said, "Let there be light," and there was light.*

—Genesis 1:3

In *Nine Lenses on the World: The Enneagram Perspective*, Jerome Wagner humorously says that every Achiever secretly wants the following epitaph written on their tombstone: "She accomplished much in a short amount of time."[2] Achievers make it look easy, possessing an effortless hustle, a "power to produce," that can amaze their friends, family, and co-workers. This God-given attribute is a reflection of the Divine's own efficaciousness, the innate ability for God's power to bring to pass whatever He desires.

> The only way to be productive is to realize that you don't have to be productive.
>
> —Matthew Perman[1]

This efficaciousness was on full display in the act of creation. With merely a word, light is spoken into existence, followed by the rest of creation—including human beings. The power of God's word is a recurring theme in Scripture, such as when God tells the prophet Isaiah: "So

1 Matthew Perman, *What's Best Next Study Guide: How the Gospel Transforms the Way You Get Things Done*, Kindle, Enlarged ed. (Zondervan, 2014), 14.

2 Jerome Wagner, *Nine Lenses on the World: The Enneagram Perspective*, Kindle ed. (NineLens Press, 2010).

shall my word be that goes out from my mouth; it shall not return to me empty, but it shall accomplish that which I purpose, and shall succeed in the thing for which I sent it."[3]

Achievers imitate God's effectiveness in this way, often bringing about impressive results with seemingly very little effort. But this "power to produce" can easily turn self-centered. Adam and Eve took the fruit—hoping to achieve by their own effort what God was trying to offer freely. Likewise, Achievers can use their gifts to draw attention to themselves: taking for themselves what has already been offered for the life of the world. The result is always disastrous.

When you buy into the Enemy's lie that deferring to God will somehow rob you of the acceptance you seek—you stretch the boundaries of what is humanely possible. As a result, you find yourself burnt out, lonely, and eventually full of despair. Production for its own sake (or for your own sake) comes at a cost, one felt most keenly by those we love.

> You are loved for who you are in Christ, not for what you do.

***The Good News for Achievers*** is that God is not asking you to be like Him in this way. He's not asking you to do everything, but to be a certain person in everything you do. He asks you to rest from labor—just as He did—and recognize that slow-burning values like honesty, commitment, and relationships are infinitely more important than anything that could be accomplished alone. The path of growth begins with admitting the difficult truth that you are neither indispensable nor untiring. So carry on "getting stuff done" (and look good while doing it), but refuse to listen to that inner voice pushing you to do more for acceptance. You are loved for who you are in Christ, not for what you do. Accept the gift of acceptance and use your gifts to produce—and then rest in the knowledge that God is still on the throne.

---

3 Isa. 55:11

### → Pray

Father, forgive me for having an inflated view of myself. I erroneously believe that everything will fall apart if I stop moving, but You hold the world in the palm of Your hand, and only by Your Holy Spirit are individual hearts and minds transformed. You can change the world without me but You've chosen to use me still. Enable me to restfully work today as I remember that my worth is found in Christ alone, not in what I produce.

# Day 7 Reflections

**What is fueling your desire to accomplish all you want to get done today?**

**How does it feel to know God won't love you any more or less in regard to how much you accomplish today?**

**What do you want the message on your tombstone to say?**

## → Respond

Write down a few personal goals that stretch beyond work.

*Day 8:*

# Love Trumps Productivity

*If I speak in the tongues of men and of angels, but have not love, I am a noisy gong or a clanging cymbal.*

—1 Corinthians 13:1

---

ACHIEVERS ARE CONSUMMATE PRODUCERS. FOR YOU, THE world is a disorganized, undeveloped mess just waiting for someone to swoop in and create order. Not only do you streamline organizations, create high-functioning teams, and increase productivity, it's done with style—often with awards and accolades following.

Even with the increased productivity, those who work with Achievers commonly feel a creeping sense of insufficiency. When these heroes of order and efficiency encounter team members who seem to lag behind, they often become impatient, frustrated, or overtly hostile (when output is not matching potential).

> Love people the way Jesus loves you.
>
> –Anonymous

This passion for perfection and productivity mirrors the Divine's artistic form. Remember, in the act of creation God said His world was very good. But for Achievers to most accurately reflect the Imago Dei, they must not only produce quality, but must also slow down enough to appreciate the journey. While it's true that God called Adam and Eve to steward creation, to fill, subdue, and rule over the earth, all of it is to be done in the context of a loving relationship with God and others. The true beauty of stewardship is not mastery of a product, but the relationships forged in the process.

As with Christ's Life, the quality—the "very good-ness"—is not primarily the destination, some "sweet by and by," but in the relationship. Life after death is only a good motivator if we experience life before death: the hereafter is colored by the shades of our relationships in the here-and-now. Jesus' work not only set captives free for all eternity, but in the midst of their every day lives and relationships. The Apostle Paul tells the Corinthians all of their great works will be as "noisy gongs" if they are not shot through with the greatest part of God's image: love. And Jesus tells the religious leaders that until they love their neighbors, they do not really love God, no matter their piety.

> The true beauty of stewardship is the relationships forged in the process.

***The Good News for Achievers*** is that your definition for "success" can be reworked to reflect the image of God. Slowing down can offer the opportunity to love and instill every relationship with the sort of life Christ came to bring. Even if a particular project has to take the back seat, reorienting priorities around love and relationship over ruthless efficiency will draw others to you in the long run. The true definition of success is developing a loyal team built on trust that will be able to tackle increasingly difficult and intricate work because of their mutual love for one another.

### → Pray

Father, You created me so that I might know You, but I lose my way when I believe I'm only useful to You when achieving. Forgive me for being so overly focused on what I need to do that I forget who is with me. Help me take my eyes off myself and my goals to be present with You and others. Enable me by Your Holy Spirit to be productively loving.

# Day 8 Reflections

**Through whom have you experienced God's love the most? Is their love conditional on your performance?**

**If someone asked you to do less today to be with people more, what would you say?**

**How will your day look different knowing God values love over productivity?**

## → Respond

List the names of three or four people and write down one way to productively love them today (e.g. quality time, giving a gift, word of encouragement, ask what they need help with, etc.).

## *Day 9:*

# Misplaced Identity

*For you have died, and your life is hidden with Christ in God. When Christ who is your life appears, then you also will appear with him in glory.*

—Colossians 3:3-4

---

We are all attracted to success in one way or another. The desire to cozy up to those who have apparently cracked the "get along and get ahead" code is built into our DNA and is what has enabled human society to progress as it has. Without successful, charismatic leaders, it would be difficult to unite such diverse people to work toward a common cause.

> If our identity is in our work, rather than Christ, success will go to our heads, and failure will go to our hearts.
>
> –Timothy Keller

If they are not the leaders, Achievers are most often found among the company of the successful and prestigious. The most sensitive will even be able to identify those who will soon be on top, and will become the "early adopters," climbing on the bus to see how far it takes them. Again, while it is natural to seek those who are (or will be) successful, difficulties arise when Achievers confuse their own identity with the leader, organization, or brand. But as much as your personal or team successes may be part of you, they are not you. The lie Achievers are especially vulnerable to is that people are only as good as their last success or as bad as their last failure.

But Jesus offers another way. He invites us to stop basing our self-esteem and personal value on the changeable successes and failures of our daily pursuits and instead find our worth in those immutable characteristics we've been given as sharers in the Divine image. For example, Jesus promises that those who build their house on the rock will live secure but those who build their house on the sand will be swept away. Fortune's swiftly turning wheel can find even the most accomplished people and groups on the bottom in almost no time. If your identity is based upon a shifting thing like accolades, productivity, or wealth, you can soon find your self-worth swept away with what remains of your successes.

> The lie Achievers believe is that they are only as good as their last success.

But it doesn't have to be this way.

***The Good News for Achievers*** is when we trust in Christ, building our lives upon His solidity and finding our identity securely hidden within Him, He becomes both our solid rock and tower of refuge. More than any other type, you know the drive to get to the top, the elation of making it there, and the soul-eating envy of watching others make it instead. But Jesus astoundingly offers us His success over sin, death, and the accuser's lies as a free gift no matter how big of a success or failure we are. When Achievers find their identity in Christ, it levels the playing field for those on the top and the bottom of society's ladder of success. This displays all of us as the children and images of God we were made to be, protected forever from both condemnation and separation from His unconditional love.

### → Pray

Father, I have found myself searching for self-worth in the things the world sees as successful. Forgive me for all the ways I have tried to build my reputation on the sands of changing outward approval. Thank You for sending Your Son to go to the cross. Without any protection, He received the condemnation for sin that I deserved so that He might be my rock of protection.

# Day 9 Reflections

**Who are you apart from your success or successful associations?**

**What can you do today to claim that your success is in Christ alone and de-emphasize your identification with your own accomplishments?**

## → Respond

Search for, listen to, and meditate on the words of this hymn: "My Hope Is Built On Nothing Less (Christ The Solid Rock)."

*Day 10:*

# Fear of Being Mediocre

*And when he came up out of the water, immediately he saw the heavens being torn open and the Spirit descending on him like a dove. And a voice came from heaven, "You are my beloved Son; with you I am well pleased."*

—Mark 1:10-11

---

ANOTHER WORD ACHIEVERS RUN FROM IS "ORDINARY." Though no one wants to be forgettable, some people live under constant belief they must become a somebody. Pop legend Madonna once shared in a Vanity Fair interview:

> My drive in life is from this horrible fear of being mediocre. And that's always pushing me, pushing me. Because even though I've become Somebody, I still have to prove that I'm Somebody. My struggle has never ended and it probably never will.[1]

> I won't be happy till I'm as famous as God.
>
> –Madonna

Do you resonate with this struggle of wanting to be a somebody? Have you found your happiness depending on your current successes? Do you ever hope to feel like you've

---

1 Lynn Hirschberg, "The Misfit," Vanity Fair, April 1, 1991, https://archive.vanityfair.com/article/share/bd86a835-b84c-47a7-bbec-60b9af6ea282

arrived—that you can finally rest, basking in the glow of your achievement—or do you immediately get back on the treadmill and begin the hunt all over again?

Popular culture insists that our value is tied to the qualities that can foster success, whether they be physical, or related to our title, wealth, or connections. None of these attributes are in and of themselves bad, and while some are natural, others are won through hard work—but they are fleeting. What the God who gave these gifts freely offers is a more sure source of value, a source based not on what we can achieve but simply through who we are.

When Jesus is baptized early in His ministry—before He has accomplished much of anything—the skies open and He hears the affirming voice of the Father reminding Him just how valuable He was. This affirmation is not given because of the act itself (the Father already felt this way about Him), but the drama of submission to His will gives the Father opportunity to remind those with ears to hear just who Jesus is: a beloved Son of the Source of all.

You, too, are offered many reminders of the eternal acceptance of this same Source. The faith based on that same affirming Father built in many ways (such as baptism) to remind God's forgetful children of their eternal belovedness. Just as a parent holds their newborn child in a gaze of sheer delight and acceptance long before they have done anything worthy of love, so too does the Father gaze at you. It is up to us to remember, whether in the baptistry or walking with our fellow forgetful brothers and sisters, all of whom are filled with the same light that shined upon Christ that day in the river.

> Heaven will not be filled with people who have the most impressive resumes.

***The Good News for Achievers***—whether those chasing the next opportunity to be a somebody or those eternally frustrated by the pursuit—is that heaven will not be filled with people who have the most impressive resumes. Rather, it will be filled with people who cast the crown of their successes at the feet of Jesus crying out, "Worthy are you, our Lord and God, to receive glory and honor and power";[2]

2 Revelation 4:11

it will be filled with those who have made it their business to achieve constant remembrance of their God-given worth rather than never-ending success.

### → Pray

Father, only You are worthy. Forgive me for using the incredible talents You've given me to make myself famous. I've put myself on the throne where only You deserve to be, but Your Son placed Himself on the cross to say, "No more!" to such striving. Open my ears today to hear Your affirming voice coming through the clouds so that I might minister out of Your love and not for Your love.

# Day 10 Reflections

**How does knowing you are already a "somebody" in God's eyes change the reason you do anything today?**

**To what extent does the fear of being a "nobody" keep you on the success treadmill?**

**What would change about you if you lived your life with absolutely nothing to prove?**

## → Respond

Go spend some time today with someone who might not be viewed as "successful" in the eyes of the world.

## *Day 11:*

# People Are Not Obstacles

*Then children were brought to him that he might lay his hands on them and pray. The disciples rebuked the people, but Jesus said, "Let the little children come to me and do not hinder them, for to such belongs the kingdom of heaven." And he laid his hands on them and went away."*

—Matthew 19:13-15

---

The legacy of your life will not be judged by how many emails you responded to… It will be measured, I believe, by how interruptible you were.

–Jeff Goins[1]

THE DRAW TO BE CONSTANTLY CONNECTED AND "reachable" is strong, often carrying with it implications for a person's success in our highly competitive society. Yet oddly enough, Achievers rarely feel frustrated by the dings and blinking notifications on their phones—those make Achievers feel more successful. It's the people who interrupt that make life difficult.

1 Jeff Goins, "Please, Interrupt Me: Why We Need Interruptions to Grow," Goins, Writer, August 15, 2013, https://goinswriter.com/interrupt-me/.

Whether it's inefficient meetings, easily-distracted or sluggish co-workers, or just plain small talk, it might feel as if the world is purposefully getting in your way. You may wonder at times if life's a video game and everyone you know is an antagonist, actively working to keep you from finishing the level.

In the Book of Matthew, we read that the disciples view the little children who come to Jesus as obstacles to His mission. They even go so far as to rebuke the parents for allowing their children to hinder Jesus' teaching. But when Jesus looks at these innocent, energetic, smiling faces He sees God-given opportunities. He stops what He's doing to simply be with them, to hold them in His arms and engage as though they are the most important thing in the world at that moment.

> Many people in your life have set aside time to be interrupted by you—so return the gift.

It's hard to imagine a world where interruptions in our day are a good thing, but Jesus redefines our definition of success. He was a leader who knew how to walk slowly through a crowd, who viewed the interruptions themselves as the opportunities for life—not just for the people with whom He engaged, but for Himself as well. Jesus wasn't easily-interruptible only because it was good for others, but because it gave Him life, too.

Achievers, perhaps more than any other type, tend to steer away from complicated or demanding relationships because they take time and energy to maintain. Their own and others' feelings end up on a shelf, possibly revisited at a later time because they threaten the productivity of the moment.

***The Good News for Achievers*** is that both the problem and solution are fairly easy to discover. The first step is simply to identify the problem. Ask yourself: When do I feel most frustrated? You will likely notice the moments that consistently frustrate you are uninvited interruptions. The accompanying solution is simple at the beginning: Take a deep breath and allow the distraction to occur.

Remember, many people in your life have willingly and consistently set aside time to be interrupted by you—so return the gift. Of course, a healthy life includes boundaries (even Jesus made for work and rest), but the first step is to begin being interruptible, rather than spending a whole life frustrated by what happens naturally. Learn to walk slowly through a crowd and wonder at the many "innocent ones" God sets in your path.

### → Pray

Father, You have always been willing to be "interrupted" by Your children. Forgive me for seeing other beings filled with Your Spirit as distractions. Forgive me for being socially-selective and avoiding people I think will take too much of my time. Change my daily scorecard from getting the most tasks done to simply being present with whomever You put in my path.

# Day 11 Reflections

**How does Jesus' challenge our understanding of productivity?**

**Do you have a strategy for avoiding time-consuming conversations or high-maintenance relationships? How would embracing those help you grow more?**

**What is one way you can make yourself more accessible to others?**

## → Respond

When you are interrupted today, welcome the detour as a divine appointment. Notice what happens when you change your perspective.

## *Day 12:*

# Living for Others' Eyes

*For am I now seeking the approval of man, or of God? Or am I trying to please man? If I were still trying to please man, I would not be a servant of Christ.*

—Galatians 1:10

WOULD YOU DO SOMETHING YOU HATE IN order to be successful? Andre Agassi, one of the greatest tennis players of all time, said, "I play tennis for a living even though I hate tennis, hate it with a dark and secret passion and always have." In his autobiography, *Open*, he spoke of a father who was unable to "tell the difference between loving me and loving tennis."[1] After winning his first Grand Slam title at Wimbledon in 1992, his father's first response was, "You had no business losing that fourth set."[2]

> If you live for people's acceptance you will die from their rejection.
>
> –Lecrae

What drove Agassi to succeed was not a love for tennis but a desire to win the love of his hard-to-please father. Much like the tennis legend, Achievers will do almost anything to secure the sense of worth they so crave, even if

1 Agassi, *Open*, 202.

2 Associated Press, "Andre Agassi Writes of Hatred of Father, Tennis in Upcoming Autobiography," ESPN.com (ESPN, October 29, 2009), https://www.espn.com/sports/tennis/news/story?id=4603632.

they know the person or people to whom they've given this power will never offer complete and lasting acceptance. As Riso and Hudson explain, "[Achievers] want to make sure their lives are a success, however that is defined by their family, their culture, and their social sphere."[3]

The story of Roman governor Pontius Pilate vividly illustrates the tension between pleasing man and God. Although Pilate is under great stress (he personally has to speak to the Emperor for any unrest in his province), he nevertheless chooses what he knows to be the wrong path, simply to avoid trouble. He meets Jesus face to face and knows this strange rabbi is innocent. He asks the crowds point-blank: "What has he done wrong?" (Mark 15:14), but as the voices grow louder, the fear of failure increases. He has a decision to make: lose the approval of the crowd and possibly the Emperor, or allow Jesus to die and win their favor?[4]

> When we give others the key to our value we will never find rest.

When we're seeking someone's approval and their voices grow loud in our lives, we succumb to the pressure of their desires for us. The truth is, we may win their favor for a time—but there's always a price. Achievers so badly need the approval that comes with a job well done. However, when we give others the key to our value—when they hold the power to extend or withhold our worth—we will never find rest, even in the midst of our greatest successes.

***The Good News for Achievers*** is that our ultimate worth is held in the One who made us—and He never changes. Our worth is secure in Him. Without Him, our source of life, no amount of success will bring peace. But, in God, we will find peace that no amount of success or failure can shake.

---

3 The Enneagram Institute, "Type Three," The Enneagram Institute, 2019, https://www.enneagraminstitute.com/type-3.

4 cf. Luke 23:23-25

### → Pray

Father, You are Lord over all, and You will not give your glory to another. Your son Jesus came not to do the will of others, but Your will alone. Your approval of me is secure because I am Your child. Forgive me for all the time I've spent fixated on how to impress others. Help me to be a true servant who finds my ultimate worth in You alone.

# Day 12 Reflections

**Do you tend to make decisions because God puts an idea in your heart or someone else?**

**What expectations do the people in your life have of you? What would happen if you became convinced that pleasing God meant going in a different direction?**

## → Respond

Take a day for solitude. Silence the voices around you, and write down what you sense God calling you to do.

## *Day 13:*

# Inefficient Productivity

*For we are his workmanship, created in Christ Jesus for good works, which God prepared beforehand, that we should walk in them.*

—Ephesians 2:10

---

TECHNOLOGY WRITER COLIN ROBINSON ONCE DISCUSSED THE difference between *efficiency* and *effectiveness*. He explained that many people are great at being *efficient*: completing many tasks quickly and with little effort. But like using a high-efficiency LED porch light during the day, their efficiency didn't lead to tangible effects. It may be wise to replace an old incandescent bulb with LED light bulb, but its light is only useful in the dark.

> The most unproductive thing of all is to make more efficient what should not be done at all.
>
> –Peter Drucker

Achievers are confident, hard-working people who—given the right context—can turn their drive and effortless efficiency into actual *effectiveness*. Being *efficient* is about "doing things right," but being *effective* is about "doing the right things." In other words, checking off the most tasks with the least amount of time and energy may just mean extra space to do more of the wrong things.

Not only are Achievers inwardly driven to feel like they are conquering their tasks, but such charismatic, high-energy performers will always be in high demand by the people around them. Having the potential to do many things well often leaves Achievers feeling pressure to do what others want on top of their own tasks. But we are called to be driven differently, listening to God's desires and direction for us.

> Being efficient is about "doing things right," but being effective is about "doing the right things."

So how do you know what tasks have been given from God and which ones are passing interests? What are the things we have been called to do with *effectiveness,* and what would we merely be *efficient* in? God promises us that works done in His name are not in vain, but how do we know when we're actually doing those works in His name and not our own? It's easy to simply say, "listen to God and walk in the works He's prepared for you," but how do we *know*?

Jesus could have become more efficient in His ministry, optimized His ministry for the greatest impact in the works of healing, feeding, and teaching, or followed the crowds' desire to become a king. But He denied these wishes and fled from them, even going so far as to promise His disciples that *they*, not He, would do the greater works. That was because the good works He accomplished were not His true task but stopping points on the way to Jerusalem, where He would do the one work that had been prepared for Him by the Father.

***The Good News for Achievers*** is that we have the Spirit of Jesus to help us discern the path of most effectiveness. We may not be able to see the current of the river of God's will, but it is not difficult to feel when we are swimming with or against it. Frederick Buechner wrote that "The place God calls you to is the place where your deep gladness and the world's deep hunger meet."[1] God's calling on our lives doesn't mean we efficiently accomplish things that aren't really important or that we wait in tortured uncertainty for a voice from heaven. Rather, we are called to stop and take a purposeful look at our possibilities. God speaks through our

---

1 Frederick Buechner, *Wishful Thinking*, (London, Mowbray, 1994), 119.

skills, interests, and other people with whom we could partner in good works. He speaks in the silence we allow so we can listen and in the peace that comes when our work flows from *efficiency* into *effectiveness.*

### → Pray

Father, forgive us for working expediently so we can brag about how much we get done. Help us to slow down enough to delight in Your Word and meditate on Your ways to understand Your definition of success.

# Day 13 Reflections

**How did Jesus pursue effectiveness over efficiency in His ministry?**

**How might you sense the current of God's will in order to accomplish tasks to which you've truly been called?**

**What or who are you avoiding by accomplishing so much?**

**To be more effective, what are you doing efficiently that you should be delegating?**

## → Respond

Write a 50-word personal mission statement that will help you prioritize your future pursuits.

## *Day 14:*

# Only Half Listening

*Know this, my beloved brothers: let every person be quick to hear, slow to speak, slow to anger.*

—James 1:19

---

EACH OF US HAVE BEEN GIVEN A ministry of both doing and listening. As pastor David Mathis says, "The best ministry you might do today is to listen to someone's pain all the way to the bottom."[1] The future-orientated doer in you will always make it a challenge to listen with both ears in the present moment.

> He who can no longer listen to his brother will soon be no longer listening to God either.
>
> –Dietrich Bonhoeffer

The desire to move on, to "get stuff done," may lead others to experience you as impatient and rushed or even inauthentic; Achievers often pretend to be interested in conversations when they truly aren't.[2] Inefficient or less-competent people often receive less of your attention, and you'll find yourself formulating a quick response while others are still talking.

---

1 David Matthis, "Six Lessons in Good Listening," Desiring God, April 3, 2014, https://www.desiringgod.org/articles/six-lessons-in-good-listening.

2 Cron and Stabile, *The Road*, 135.

The quick-thinking and "always on" traits are part of what makes you both effective and efficient, but your clear, bullet-pointed communication often gives away more than you intend. This quickness to move on can also be a defense mechanism: when the conversation becomes painful, it's not hard to signal you are ready to move on.[3] This defense will not only keep you from plumbing the depths of others' pain, it will also alienate you from your own.

Enneagram expert Suzanne Stabile offers this warning to Achievers:

> You may be impatient or dismissive with someone who wants to be heard, like a Six, or with someone who processes verbally, like a Two. Threes [Achievers] are often intolerant of darker emotions, but unless Threes can learn to be present to the other person's feelings and their own, the relationship will surely be compromised."[4]

> Through good listening we invite others to understand just how much they matter apart from what they do.

It's true that many appreciate the "love through doing" approach, but developing the art of being present, of listening "to the bottom" will make you much more effective in your projects and in life. We are, after all, human beings, not human doings. As God's image-bearers, we are not called to represent His efficaciousness only, but also His loving presence. This means we are called to be "quick to listen" as James says (1:19). Through good listening and dwelling in the present, we invite others to understand just how much they matter apart from what they do.

***The Good News for Achievers*** is that opportunities for practice abound. Most of the time, what you are working on is not in the "urgent-important" category, so become interruptible. When someone speaks with you, inhabit that moment with them. Sometimes, all that's necessary to fix the problem is to give people the opportunity to express themselves. Try asking more open-ended questions that don't give you the opportunity to move on too quickly. Although you might look

---

3 Integrative9 Enneagram Solutions, "Enneagram Test for Coaching and Leadership Development," www.integrative9.com, 2020, https://www.integrative9.com/.

4 Suzanne Stabile, *The Path Between Us: An Enneagram Journey to Healthy Relationships*, Kindle edition (IVP Books, 2018), 105.

back at your day and remember what you achieved, others might look back at their conversation with you with gratitude because you were present when they needed you. Ultimately, these are the works that remain.

### → Pray

Father, Your eyes are on the righteous and Your ears are attentive to their prayers. You promise that if we confess our sin[5] and ask anything according to Your will, You surely listen. Forgive me for not being attentive to Your voice throughout the day, even though You are always speaking. Enable me by the Spirit to be a child who is fully present with You and Your other children.

5 1 John 1:9

# Day 14 Reflections

**How has listening with half an ear affected your relationships in the past?**

**To what extent does your desire for expediency affect your ability to listen? What about your disdain for negative emotions?**

**How does the fact that Jesus withdrew often to listen to the Father challenge your understanding of a productive day?**

## → Respond

In the middle of a conversation, stop and ask someone how you can pray for them.

## *Day 15:*

# Effortless Grace

*For all have sinned and fall short of the glory of God, and are justified by his grace as a gift, through the redemption that is in Christ Jesus.*

—Romans 3:23-24

---

BECAUSE GRACE REQUIRES NOTHING OF US, IT can either be an Achiever's best friend or greatest enemy. As the Apostle Paul points out, grace and work are not mutually exclusive, but intended to be in relationship with one another: "I worked harder than any of them, though it was not I, but the grace of God that is with me."[1] Grace fuels effort, but when it comes to our salvation, grace is opposed to earning. If grace could be earned, Achievers—with their Type-A personality—would surely be ahead of everyone else in line.

> Grace is not opposed to effort, it is opposed to earning.
>
> –Dallas Willard

Receiving grace as a free gift is challenging for Achievers precisely because they are relying on someone else's achievement to do for them what could never be done on their own. To become a Christian, you must first admit all of your greatest successes are "filthy rags," full of

1 1 Cor. 15:10.

conflicting motives, and ultimately pale in comparison to God's eternally gracious offer of love. As Timothy Keller explains, "To truly become Christians we must also repent of the reasons we ever did anything right."[2]

Elsewhere, Keller also notes that many modern people seek to save themselves from the perceived hell of worthlessness and insignificance through chasing after status-upgrading opportunities. But attempting to find salvation in this way is a futile dead end. When the excitement fades, we all know every "upgrade" hasn't lived up to the hype. In addition, the status you currently enjoy could be taken away at any moment due to a moral failure, family crisis, company lay-off, public criticism, or something else unforeseen. In that moment, what past accomplishment will rescue you from the embarrassment and shame?

Receiving grace is challenging for Achievers precisely because they are relying on someone else's achievement.

***The Good News for Achievers*** is that God's justification has been offered without any work on our part. In spite of our consistent failure to act in accordance with God's perfect will, we have been brought into right relationship with our Creator.[3] Through no action of our own, we have been brought into a lasting peace with God, and the knowledge that this same gift has been offered to every piece of this broken and beautiful earth is enough to make every relationship and interaction sacred.

---

2 Timothy Keller, *The Prodigal God*, Kindle edition (Penguin Books, 2008).

3 People Launching, "Gospel Enneagram," Gospel Enneagram, 2020, https://www.gospelenneagram.com.

### → Pray

Father, I am filled with gratitude to You for doing for me what I could never do for myself. You sent Your Son, Jesus, so that I might be able to see myself as Your child. Your grace has made peace where I saw only contention before. By Your Spirit, restrain me from trying to add to the finished work of the cross through my accomplishments. Help me today to give unconditional grace to those around me.

# Day 15 Reflections

**What do you think is the look on God's face as He sees you right now?**

**In what ways have you tried to secure an "untouchable" status through your effort? What is the result of those efforts?**

**How do you treat others when they fail you? What might that reveal about your true understanding of grace?**

## → Respond

As a way to demonstrate the gospel, the next time someone drops the ball, show them grace and then offer to help.

*Day 16:*

# The Self-Promoting Peacock

*God chose what is low and despised in the world, even things that are not, to bring to nothing things that are, so that no human being might boast in the presence of God. And because of him you are in Christ Jesus, who became to us wisdom from God, righteousness and sanctification and redemption, so that, as it is written, "Let the one who boasts, boast in the Lord."*

—1 Corinthians 1:28-31

---

"PEACOCKS ARE BEAUTIFUL, BUT THEIR BEHAVIOR IS not." The headline was too strange not to read further as the wildlife columnist described the troubles these bright creatures caused to their Bay Area neighborhood. The tag went hilariously on: "Danville peacocks are causing a ruckus, pooping everywhere and destroying gardens."[1] We have to wonder if the flamboyant birds had any idea of the disruption they caused, or if they were just happy to have a place to spread their wings and … leave their mark.

> Boasting is always an advertisement of poverty.
>
> —W. Graham Scroggie

1 Joan Morris, "Peacocks Are Beautiful, but Their Behavior Is Not," The Mercury News, June 8, 2018, https://www.mercurynews.com/2018/06/08/peacocks-are-beautiful-but-their-behavior-is-not/.

In his ground-breaking Enneagram work, Franciscan priest Richard Rohr compares the "heart types" (Helpers, Achievers, and Individualists) to a peacock:

> The peacock shows himself off. His getup draws attention to him. The long-term goal of counseling for heart types must be to bundle away the peacock and to dock his tail, so that it becomes clear that without his finery he is just as much a normal, ugly chicken as the rest of us.[2]

This humorous illustration describes the desire of Achievers to show off their impressive, glorious feathers. For unhealthy Achievers, it's as though every act—no matter how apparently selfless—comes with a plea, "Please see my beautiful feathers; validate me, see me!"

While some people boast openly, other Achievers prefer to have their accolades related to them: a "vanity for having no vanity," as Beatrice Chestnut puts it.[3] They don't want to be caught bragging in obvious self-promotion, but achieve the validation they long for by becoming masters at "fishing for compliments."

> Rather than drawing attention to yourself, point the world to Someone far more glorious.

This attention-angling is often so subtle, so opposed to the obvious bragging, it hardly registers. Whether taking the form of sharing your learning, constantly updating your work progress, explaining how successful your team is, or mentioning the well-known people you work with, it can seem innocent enough. But if you find yourself feeling a little uncomfortable with that list, then you may be an Achiever who knows the underlying reason for these unsolicited updates.

In his letters to the churches of Revelation, John warns the Laodiceans, "For you say, 'I am rich, I have prospered, and I need nothing,' but you do not realize that you are wretched, pitiable, poor, blind, and naked."[4] No matter what you look like

---

2 Rohr and Ebert, *The Enneagram*, 88.

3 Chestnut, The *9 Types of Leadership*, 116.

4 Revelation 3:17

to others, whether your bragging is as loud as the Laodocieans or the subtlest humble-brag, God sees the true condition and emptiness of your heart.

Rather than throwing up the feathers today to draw attention to yourself, point the world to Someone far more glorious: Jesus, the true humble servant, who "did not count equality with God a thing to be grasped, but emptied himself."[5] The Apostle Paul goes on to explain that this emptying—*kenosis*—ultimately found its end in Christ's sacrifice at the cross. It's an attitude directly opposed to the type of emptiness validation-fishing displays. In fact, it's what made Christ uniquely and fully human. His humanity (which was more fully-realized than our own) was directly correlated to His servanthood: "He took the nature of a servant: being made in human likeness."

***The Good News for Achievers*** is that the first steps toward this emptying are straightforward. We don't have to deflect authentic, unsolicited praise, but we can begin noticing when the temptation to fish arises. When the urge to be noticed wells up, perform an act of *kenosis*—empty yourself and praise those around you (even those you suspect are fishing as well). Notice others' achievements, pour into other hearts the warm light you so greatly desire, and see if the warmth isn't reflected back.

### → Pray

Father, You are the King of glory and Your Son, Jesus, is the radiance of Your glory. Forgive me for falling short of Your glory by attempting to draw others' eyes off of You and onto myself. Empty me of all boasting and fill me with Your Spirit to open my eyes so I might see Your great works in others' lives and declare Your praises before all.

5 Philippians 2:6-7

# Day 16 Reflections

**How do you fish for compliments? In what ways do you use subtlety for self-promotion?**

**What would it look like to "empty" yourself of self-promotion and instead promote others more?**

## → Respond

Try to go the whole day without talking (or posting) about yourself. Ask someone what they've accomplished and promote them.

*Day 17:*

# Cutting Corners

*Now Samuel had died, and all Israel had mourned for him and buried him in Ramah, his own city. And Saul had put the mediums and the necromancers out of the land... Then Saul said to his servants, "Seek out for me a woman who is a medium, that I may go to her and inquire of her..."*

—1 Samuel 28:3, 7

---

ACHIEVERS ARE TEMPTED TO CUT CORNERS WHEN efficiency and productivity are of ultimate concern. In this state, the ends always justify the means. The Achiever might do something questionably bad to accomplish what seems unquestionably good to them. Biblical commands, ethical principles, and values may get substituted for a "whatever works" mentality. Suzanne Stabile points out that they may even have trouble expressing consistent personal values because the chameleon tendency is to fit in with whatever group they are with.[2]

> The end justifies the means.
>
> –Three Proverb[1]

But your intensity must not outpace your integrity. The drive to achieve cannot

1 Wagner, *Nine Lenses*.

2 Stabile, *The Path Between Us*, 102.

overshadow your values. To have integrity is to be undivided between stated values and behavior, even (or especially) when the cost is high. The biblical story of Daniel is a study in integrity. When Jerusalem falls to Nebuchadnezzar, he is exiled to Babylon where he joins other promising Hebrew youth in the conquering king's court. Despite the pressure to conform and rise through the ranks, he maintains the values of his God. He is even willing to be thrown to the lions rather than compromise his obedience.[3]

> Your intensity must not outpace your integrity.

King Saul is a different story. Right after the Prophet Samuel's death, the Philistine army is approaching the Israelites and Saul becomes desperate to know whether he could defeat them. Because of Saul's past disobedience, God had chosen not to speak to him any more. Saul panics and decides to secretly visit a medium, despite having recently banished all such practices from the land. Desperate to hear from the Lord, he pays a witch to summon the departed prophet's spirit, who predicts not an Israelite victory, but defeat and death for Saul.[4]

***The Good News for Achievers*** is that Jesus did not cut any corners on His mission to rescue us, and in maintaining His integrity to the end, He opened the way to hope and new life. Though Satan tempted Jesus in the wilderness with multiple short cuts,[5] Jesus's mission could not be eased. He, like Daniel and Saul, was offered no certainty and bravely faced death for His commitment to God's ways. Despite the fear and pain, both found life by following their callings to the end: Daniel was rescued from the lions and Jesus opened our eyes to God's love through the cross and rising to a new, unending life. Today, choose the narrow path of integrity which, though full of darkness and doubt, leads to peace and the real life Christ came to bring.

---

3 Daniel 6

4 I Samuel 28

5 cf. Matthew 4:1-11

### → Pray

Father, You do not change like shifting shadows. You are the same yesterday, today, and forever. Forgive me for shape-shifting and cutting corners on the things You value the most. Keep me from compromising with evil and fill me with joy as I walk in integrity with Your people.

# Day 17 Reflections

**When are you tempted to cut corners?**

**How does the gospel motivate you to do "the right thing the right way," no matter the cost?**

**How will you put accountability measures in place to keep you from compromising in the future?**

## → Respond

Make a list of the values you want to be associated with (e.g. loyalty, generosity, patience, integrity, etc.).

*Day 18:*

# Aerodynamic Leadership

*Do you not know that in a race all the runners run, but only one receives the prize? So run that you may obtain it. Every athlete exercises self-control in all things. They do it to receive a perishable wreath, but we an imperishable. So I do not run aimlessly; I do not box as one beating the air. But I discipline my body and keep it under control, lest after preaching to others I myself should be disqualified.*

—1 Corinthians 9:24-27

---

> Aerodynamic leaders, by design, seek to elevate or lift those around them.
>
> –Toby Edwards[1]

THE WRIGHT BROTHERS NEVER COULD HAVE IMAGINED how their first flight at Kitty Hawk in 1903 would speed up the world. Within decades, humans were no longer constrained by the difficulties of traveling over land or sea, but could cover the entire breadth of continents and oceans in a matter of hours.

1 Toby Edwards, "Radiology Management, ICU Management, Healthcare IT, Cardiology Management, Executive Management," HealthManagement, 2020, https://healthmanagement.org/c/healthmanagement/issuearticle/aerodynamic-leadership.

Just as these masters of flight ushered in a world in which we can accomplish more than ever before, Achievers are leaders who can increase the productivity of everyone working with them. Like seasoned pilots, a healthy Achiever sits in the cockpit, casting vision for what's ahead. They adjust flight plans to avoid storms, know what to do in a crisis, and keep staff and passengers confident in achieving the goal.

Many Achievers reflect this aerodynamic quality, almost possessing a "sixth sense" for whether a particular action will help move you or your team toward the goal. As one experienced "pilot" shared,

> "People are amazed how I put things into perspective and stay on track. When people around the district are stuck on issues and caught on contrived barriers, I am able to pole-vault over them, reestablish the focus, and keep things moving."[2]

The Apostle Paul emphasizes this kind of leadership to the congregation in Ephesus, reminding these believers that the gospel advances when spiritual leaders have the self-discipline of an athlete, the work ethic of a farmer, and the focus of a soldier.[3] When we lose sight of our lives and switch on the auto-pilot, we become lazy and undisciplined, which will be reflected in those we are trying to lead. An Achiever on auto-pilot is even more dangerous than most, because people will follow you, even when you're going nowhere!

> A healthy Achiever sits in the cockpit, casting vision for what's ahead.

Others may not naturally sort through conflicting priorities, find more efficient ways of doing things, or invent new systems and routines to help projects run more smoothly, but God has given you a large measure of tenacity, drivenness, and determination to lead His people, if you will seize this power well.

***The Good News for Achievers*** is that Jesus offers direction for the stewardship of your gifts. He lived an undistracted life of self-control, focus, and determination.

---

2 Marcus Buckingham and Donald O Clifton, *Now, Discover Your Strengths: How to Develop Your Talents and Those of the People You Manage* (London: Pocket Books, 2005), 99.

3 2 Tim. 2:1-7

Jesus dedicated His life to serving, ultimately focused on fulfilling His task at the cross—setting people free from their self-deceit to step into God's waiting, loving arms. Because of the Holy Spirit within each of us, we can throw off the obstacles that hinder us to run the race well and help others to do the same.

### → Pray

Father, You are the wise King, but when I don't acknowledge Your rule I drift toward wasting my time by doing what is right in my own eyes. Forgive me for abusing the gift of time. While I cannot get back the time I've already spent poorly, by your Holy Spirit I can re-focus my priorities to align with Yours. I can use my leadership gifts to equip the next generation of leaders.

# Day 18 Reflections

**What are the urgent but unimportant things hindering your stewardship of time?**

**How can you help the people around you become more focused and self-disciplined?**

## → Respond

Plan and lead a goal-setting meeting for your family or team.

## *Day 19:*

# The Work Affair

*And in the morning, behold, it was Leah! And Jacob said to Laban, "What is this you have done to me? Did I not serve with you for Rachel? Why then have you deceived me?"*

—Genesis 29:25

---

"Work-life balance" is one of the most difficult challenges for any Achievers to master. For these committed laborers, Jesus might as well have said, "Where your work is, there your heart will be also." Relationships, hobbies, and even personal health can take a back seat to work, leading to an addiction that is actually applauded in our culture. "Workaholism" is a common word because it's a common issue, one we barely hide our pride in. As rapper 50 Cent once bragged, "There's no rehab for success, or I'd go check in right now."[2]

> A Three's heart is in his or her work.
>
> —Helen Palmer[1]

How do know if you're addicted? Ask yourself the following questions:

---

1 Helen Palmer, *The Enneagram in Love and Work: Understanding Your Intimate and Business Relationships* (HarperOne, 2010).

2 Shaheem Reid, "50 Cent Admits To Being A Junkie: 'I'm Addicted To Success,'" MTV News (Viacom International, 2008), http://www.mtv.com/news/1601098/50-cent-admits-to-being-a-junkie-im-addicted-to-success/.

- How much energy do you reserve after work to socialize?
- Are your conversations with others mostly about what you are working on?
- Are you too tired to spend quality time with your friends or family?
- Are you consistently arriving late or cancelling important events for work?
- Are you happier at work than at home? Do you feel more engaged talking about projects with co-workers than about life with your primary relationships?[3]

If the answer to many of these questions is yes, then it's possible that your relationship with work has become a barrier to your relationships with people. Working hard can blind us to others' lives.

> God rested from His work.

Meet Jacob, a man madly in love with the young Rachel. He offers to work for her father for seven years to marry her. Though her father, Laban, agrees to the union, Jacob is so consumed with working for Rachel that he completely misses what is happening around him—including any cues that perhaps Laban isn't totally on-board with giving his younger daughter in marriage before the older, Leah, has been properly tended to.

So, on Jacob and Rachel's wedding night, the trickster pulls a fast one on his famously shifty son-in-law, and Jacob sleeps with Leah. He doesn't catch his error until the morning light reveals that "Behold, it was Leah!"

Achievers often become so consumed with their goals, they can end up years down the road with only one meaningful union left—their work. And that relationship is entirely one-sided. Like an illicit affair, an unhealthy bond with work will become all consuming until all that is left is a smoking wreckage of both work and human relationships.

Suzanne Stabile explains this danger in her book *The Path Between Us*:

---

3 Jacquelyn Smith and Erin McDowell, "15 Ways Your Job Is Destroying Your Marriage," Business Insider, 2019, https://www.businessinsider.com/signs-your-job-is-ruining-your-marriage-2016-3#realizing-that-you-are-happier-at-work-than-you-are-at-home-and-feel-more-engaged-with-your-work-colleagues-than-with-your-spouse-14.

> What serves Threes well professionally can be disastrous to personal relationships. When Threes regularly go to work early and stay late, their relationships suffer. When they consistently miss their children's activities because of projects or work, relationships suffer. If they aren't present with those they love, both physically and emotionally, relationships suffer."[4]

God rested from His work, and we can learn that rhythm from Him if we are able to separate ourselves long enough from striving and achieving to feel it. Much like the Sabbath, humans were not created for work, but work for human kind.

***The Good News for Achievers*** is that the Father is a fountain of living water, able to fill even the most broken vessels of our life. We may have starved ourselves and those around us of real presence, but God is able to mend the cracks we've created through these lower-priority relationships so that we can again fill and be filled by those to whom we've committed our lives.

### → Pray

Father, You are the Giver of meaningful work, but I have misused this gift. Forgive me for alienating myself from You and those I love the most. Help me to love with my whole heart, soul, mind, and strength through my love of other people, not just my work.

4 Stabile, *The Path Between Us*, 105.

# Day 19 Reflections

**When has your work gone from being good to being a god?**

**How has your vocation affected your relationships?**

**How does a healthy relationship with God create healthier relationships and work habits?**

## → Respond

Schedule blocks of time during the week when you absolutely will not work—and stick to it.

*Day 20:*

# Fulfillment in (Un)finished Work

*So I hated life, because the work that is done under the sun was grievous to me. All of it is meaningless, a chasing after the wind.*

—Ecclesiastes 2:17

---

DO YOU FIND IT FRUSTRATING WHEN YOU are unable to accomplish all that you want to get done? While Achievers are able to accomplish much, they are rarely are satisfied with the results, so the chase for contentment and the hope for rest in labor can seem as far away as the horizon.

> You will not have a meaningful life without work, but you cannot say that your work is the meaning of your life.
>
> –Timothy Keller[1]

Meet Niggle, a character by *The Lord of the Rings* author J.R.R. Tolkien. His pseudo-biographical short story *Leaf by Niggle* follows its protagonist as he aspires to paint a Great Tree, beginning with a single leaf. Over time the work expands, but it never seems any nearer to completion—

1 Timothy Keller and Katherine Leary Alsdorf, *Every Good Endeavor: Connecting Your Work to God's Work* (New York: Penguin Books, 2016), 40.

he is "distracted" by the necessities of life (fixing his house, tending to his sad garden, and helping his neighbor).

One day Niggle becomes sick and never returns to his painting. By the end of his life, he complains that his work is not finished. But he must leave it behind. As he "moves on" to the heavenly country, he encounters The Tree. It is unmistakably his work, but in this place he finds it as he meant it to be, better even—perfected.

Though written in the 1930s, Tolkien's tale still has relevance today. As Timothy Keller points out in his book *Every Good Endeavor*, Niggle's struggle is an Achiever's struggle. You may have aspirations of accomplishing much during your lifetime. You see so much potential like Niggle—a "grand tree" in your head. But then life happens. Things come up. Important things like loving your neighbor in need. Frustration over these apparent "setbacks" may cause you to despair as you struggle to produce what feels like a leaf's worth of work. Then you throw up your hands and lament along with the Teacher: "Everything is meaningless!"[2]

> Don't do more than God is asking you to do right now.

Do you feel like there is so much left to do that is still unfinished? Do you get angry at the lack of progress following your hard-earned labor? Does it feel as if you can never rest from your labor because you're no closer to reaching your goals than you were yesterday? The resounding wisdom from the teacher is this: Don't make work the meaning of your life. If you do, you'll get tired chasing after the wind.

***The Good News for Achievers*** is that your deepest longings will come to fruition in the life to come. So don't do more than God is asking you to do right now. Enjoy the simple things and trust that the meaning of life is found through God and in the living, not the achieving. Your small leaf, like Niggle's, is a part of a greater forest that God is cultivating even if you won't be able to see it until you reach the heavenly country. The God who began a good work in you, who will bring it to completion, will allow none of your unfinished work to be left undone in the world to come.

---

2 Pieter Collier, "Leaf by Niggle - a Symbolic Story about a Small Painter," Tolkienlibrary.com, 2005, http://www.tolkienlibrary.com/reviews/leafbyniggle.htm.

### → Pray

Father, You are the Creator who calls Your sons and daughters likewise to create and cultivate the earth. Forgive me for forgetting that You are always working when I am resting. Help me not to despair by focusing on what hasn't been done, but to find joy in what You have already done and will do.

# Day 20 Reflections

**How has your need for achievement led to discontentment? How do you view and treat others when you are discontent?**

**How can you be freed by the "meaninglessness" of your life's work?**

## → Respond

Keep a regular journal to celebrate both the small and big successes.

# *Day 21:*

# Slow Down

*For in six days the* Lord *made heaven and earth, the sea, and all that is in them, and rested on the seventh day. Therefore the* Lord *blessed the Sabbath day and made it holy.*

—Exodus 20:11

---

One afternoon I ended up on the shoulder of the interstate in my wife's Geo Prizm. Minutes before, the engine had begun making clanking noises. And soon, the poor car sputtered its last breath as I pulled off the road and remembered the oil change I'd been "meaning" to do. As an Achiever, I have found myself in situations like this many times before and naively believe that everything will work out.

> Most of the things we need to be most fully alive never come in busyness. They grow in rest.
>
> —Mark Buchanan

But it doesn't always.

Just as I figured my wife's car could keep going without an oil change, I thought I could keep going—keep achieving—without rest. But I was wrong. I kept reminding myself to take a break like I remembered to take the car into the shop: something always to be done later.

Achievers prefer not to slow down. There's no difference, really, between a Tuesday, Saturday, or a Sunday if there's work to be done. Rest, silence, solitude, or even leisure activities can become obstacles, which is why Achievers like to bring their work with them on vacations when they are supposed to be resting. It's why their phones are never far away. It's nearly impossible to log out, disconnect, and shut down.

Helen Palmer describes the daily tension:

> A project can also dominate your life. It determines priorities. It controls your time, your money, and your mind. It determines who stays in your life and who's left behind. Once committed, you can't let go. A mind split develops. The project stays with you even when you've moved to other goals. You can't dump it. You commit attention to the next step, and halfway through that step you've moved on to what's needed for the next and the next, with no stops between. You experience short bursts of anxiety when results fail to materialize... The key word is stop. It's very difficult to stop and listen to yourself once the habit takes over.[1]

> Jesus has redeemed us from being human doings.

When you ignore the "Check Engine" light in your vehicle, a breakdown typically isn't far behind. When we overwork and ignore the rhythms of life or the calls of our loved ones, burn out or physical and mental breakdowns are not far behind. As Suzanne Stabile reminds Achievers, you'll never work fast enough to "outrun your anxiety."

God knew what he was doing when He gave the command to rest, when He initiated the cycle in the act of creation itself. Life is intended to have cycles: we work, and then we rest and trust that the world will keep spinning even if we stop. This is not easy; society idolizes overwork. Most will look down on you if you are caught stealing, but laboring on a day of rest is a sign of work-ethic and commitment.

---

1 Palmer, *The Enneagram,* 91-92.

***The Good News for Achievers*** is that Jesus has redeemed us from being human doings, just as God redeemed the Israelites from being slaves in Egypt. The taskmaster's voice has been silenced, replaced with the voice that says, "Come to me, all who labor and are heavy laden, and I will give you rest."[2] In the presence of Him whose "load is easy and whose burden is light," we are freed from being overly-fixated on tasks, new ideas, goals, and what's next. Finally, we are free to rest—to be.

### → Pray

Father, You are all-powerful, all-knowing, and all-present. You never sleep or slumber. Yet You taught through example the need for a rhythm in life and for rest. Forgive me for forgetting that I am in Your image, an image in need of the Sabbath rest You've created for me. Thank You for sending Jesus to set me free from being a slave so that I might enjoy Your rest.

2 Matt. 11:28

# Day 21 Reflections

**How did Jesus slow down to be fully present with the Father and others?**

**What do you fear would happen if you took extended time off to rest? How might remembering that God never sleeps help your struggle?**

## → Respond

Do something life-giving today for pure enjoyment rather than a desired outcome.

*Day 22:*

# Starving for Solitude

*But he would withdraw to desolate places and pray.*

—Luke 5:16

---

IMAGINE WALKING INTO YOUR FAVORITE LOCAL SANDWICH shop and coming to the realization that it's a one-woman operation. She's the owner, cashier, sandwich maker, and janitor all in one. Though she's always making sandwiches for her growing number of customers, she never seems to eat. As months of lunch breaks go by, you notice she's beginning to look unhealthy. Once energetic, she now looks pale and exhausted. Though the shop has an abundance of food, she is starving herself.[1]

> You have made us for yourself, O Lord, and our heart is restless until it rests in you.
>
> –St. Augustine

Achievers have a way of satisfying others while starving themselves and those they love. When the feeling is that you are only as loved as your last success, the treadmill never stops until you collapse. Slowing down doesn't seem

1 Tim Ellmore, "The Starving Baker for Teachers," Growing Leaders, September 9, 2011, https://growingleaders.com/blog/the-starving-baker-for-teachers/. Adapted.

advantageous because it's time wasted—time spent thinking, even worrying, rather than moving closer to the next goal.

Yet Jesus practiced solitude; He spent time alone, achieving nothing. At the start of His ministry, Jesus spends 40 days fasting in the wilderness to prepare for His mission. So, He spends this incredibly vital time to do … nothing. Nothing, that is, besides silence and prayer. Before He even chooses the twelve disciples, He goes off alone to pray. Throughout His ministry, He often sneaks off to a solitary place to pray, and at the end of His life, he seeks solitude in the garden of Gethsemane.

Jesus couldn't live without solitude and neither can you.

Jesus couldn't live without solitude and neither can you. Without it, you won't be able to hear the affirming voice of the Father, understand who He made you to be, or discern what you are supposed to do. Without solitude, you may be making efficient use of your *chronos* (chronological) time but totally missing out on your *kairos* (divine moments) time that God spontaneously brings into your life. The most significant thing God might have you do today may not be on your planner.

Spiritual formation author Richard Foster recommends taking advantage of "little solitudes," such as the early morning moments in bed, drinking a cup of coffee, or sitting in traffic. Furthermore, you can designate your own "quiet place"—a special corner of a room, special chair, or find a park, church, or retreat center—whatever helps you become quiet and centered to hear the whispered words of God.

***The Good News for Achievers*** is that opportunities for solitude can be planned. As Foster says, solitude opens the door that Christ is knocking on, but the opening is up to us.[2] Thankfully, Achievers are great at setting up to-do lists! But remember, while the prioritization of time for silence and stillness is important, we shouldn't turn solitude into a "project" or try too hard to "do it successfully." Simply show up, be available, and be present. God is always ready to satisfy our hungry souls with good things.

---

2 Richard J Foster, *Celebration of Discipline: The Path to Spiritual Growth*, Kindle edition (San Francisco: HarperOne, 2018), 105–6.

### → Pray

Father, You are all-sufficient and I am not. I cannot live by bread alone; I need Your Word to survive. If Jesus depended on solitude for rest and guidance, how much more must I depend on it? Forgive me for ignoring Your knocks and resisting Your help. Feed my hungry soul and help me to find my satisfaction in You alone.

# Day 22 Reflections

**What is your greatest obstacle to practicing solitude? How would overcoming that obstacle help your long-term emotional and spiritual well-being?**

**How did Jesus use solitude to demonstrate a dependence on the Holy Spirit?**

## → Respond

Put a day of solitude on the calendar right now. On that day, plan to answer these questions: Where do I feel burdened? Where do I feel blessed? What do I feel God calling me to do? Where do I need to wait on God?

*Day 23:*

# Winning By Losing

*And Saul was very angry, and this saying displeased him. He said, "They have ascribed to David ten thousands, and to me they have ascribed thousands, and what more can he have but the kingdom?" And Saul eyed David from that day on. The next day a harmful spirit from God rushed upon Saul.*

—1 Samuel 18:8-10

---

ACHIEVERS ARE BORN INTO THE WORLD WITH the same competitive spirit Jacob had when he wrestled with his brother Esau in the womb—if there is a competition to be had, the Achiever will find it. This ingrained characteristic surfaces whether you are in your cubicle struggling to beat last month's figures or at the gym. As the saying goes, "If you're on the treadmill next to me, the answer is yes, we are racing."

> Competition brings out the best in products and the worst in people.
>
> –David Sarnoff[1]

Some people like to compete because they enjoy dominating their opponent. Achievers train, struggle, and fight for dominance for an entirely different reason. For you, this is about so much more than bragging rights or fame; it's

1 Chestnut, The *9 Types of Leadership*, 105.

a fight against shame for your own sense of self-worth. That's why Achievers often appear to be the most humble winners. Once the boost of self-worth has kicked in, they become empathetic when the loser experiences the very shame they tried so hard to avoid; if it were possible to enjoy the fruits of victory without passing along the shame of defeat, they would take it.

However, when left unchecked, the generally-positive spirit of competition can become unhealthy and lead to relational disaster. Riso and Hudson explain, "They may begin to introduce competitiveness into relationships in which it does not belong and can be highly destructive, such as parents competing with their children, or spouses with one another."[2] Like King Saul trying to skewer David after he defeated Goliath, an unchecked competitive spirit can turn sour and lead to disaster for those whose victories we should be celebrating.

Your worth is stored in a much more secure location than your win-loss columns.

Though it can be difficult to realize, the accolades and pride of victory that others (especially those close to us) receive does not come out of some finite account. Others' success does not come at our expense. But, as C.S. Lewis warned in *Mere Christianity*,

> "Pride gets no pleasure out of having something, only out of having more of it than the next man. We say people are proud of being rich, or clever, or good-looking but they are not. They are proud of being richer, or cleverer, or better-looking than others."[3]

***The Good News for Achievers*** is that you are good whether you win or lose. From the moment of creation, God has been whispering, "You are my child, my handiwork. To me, you shine like the sun, moon, and stars; like everything else I put my hand to, you are very good." While competition is a natural part of life and can be healthy, your worth is stored in a much more secure location than your win-loss columns.

---

2 Riso and Hudson, *The Wisdom*, Kindle Locations 4127-4129.

3 Keller, *Every Good Endeavor*, 117.

### → Pray

Father, Your love is unconditional and unceasing toward me even when I fail. Forgive me for the ways I use my competitiveness selfishly rather than for the benefit of others. Protect me from insecure pride and jealousy and help me to know where my worth comes from.

# Day 23 Reflections

**Richard Rohr says, "Christianity is probably the only religion in the world that teaches us, from the very cross, how to win by losing."[4] How can you show this posture in your life?**

**Who are you playing the comparison game with right now and how is it affecting your relationship?**

## → Respond

Help someone with a task or project today that you know will gain them praise from others.

4 Rohr and Ebert, *The Enneagram,* XXIII.

# *Day 24:*
# You Can't Please Everyone

*The fear of man lays a snare, but whoever trusts in the Lord is safe.*

—Proverbs 29:25

---

HAVE YOU EVER BEEN IN A SITUATION where you felt like it was impossible to please everyone? Welcome to the life of Pontius Pilate. Though we touched on his part in Christ's story earlier, it may help to know some of this Roman official's own tale. His time ruling Judea—what Rome viewed as one of its backwater, buffer provinces—starts off poorly when he sets up images of Emperor Tiberius over Judea. The Jews are not fans of graven images, so they surround his house in Caesarea for five days in a protest that culminates in Pilate threatening to destroy all of them if they do not disperse.[1]

> Fear of man is such a part of our human fabric that we should check for pulse if someone denies it.
>
> —Edward Welch

Jewish historian Josephus records another troubling episode that comes soon after. Attempting to improve his province, Pilate constructs a water supply system, but it is soon rumored that he stole the funds for his project

---

1 Helen K Bond, *Pontius Pilate in History and Interpretation* (Cambridge University Press, 1998), 52–53.

from the temple treasury. Incensed at this further sacrilege, another protest begins—but this, it leads many Jewish deaths from Roman clubs and horses.[2]

In yet another political blunder, Pilate's associate Lucius is found to be plotting a government take-over, so the hapless governor sets up golden shields everywhere as a sign of loyalty to the Emperor. But King Herod (who also served at the pleasure of the Emperor) is irate about these shields hanging on his palace and sends a complaint to the Emperor. Pilate is reprimanded for failing to keep the peace and is threatened with a loss of his governorship at the next uprising.[3] At this point in his career, it seems a near impossible task to keep Herod, the Jews, and the Emperor all happy.

> God's acceptance of us is based on something more firm than the popularity of our next decision.

One year later, Pilate finds himself across the room from an itinerant rabbi named Jesus. Outside, he can hear the uproar caused among the people by their religious leaders, but it doesn't take much of an interview for him to realize this man is innocent. Obviously, the man should be set free—but at what cost? If the people riot, then he will almost certainly be removed or even executed. Innocent people die all the time, surely one more won't make much difference if it keeps the peace in this powder keg of a province? Will it?

Scripture teaches that "fear of man" is the desire to obey another human being over God's clear guidance when we believe they have the power to shame, reject, or threaten us. It's submitting ourselves to those who may laugh at or embarrass, abandon, oppress, or abuse us. The Book of Proverbs says that when this fear becomes our primary motivator, it will become a trap and cause us to feel paralyzed and second-guess all of our decisions due to others' critiques and judgments.

---

2 Bond, *Pontius Pilate*, 53.

3 Charles D. Yonge, trans. *The Works of Philo Judaeus, the Contemporary of Josephus*, United Kingdom: H. G. Bohn, 1854, 165-166.

But molding our decisions after others' desires is always a short-term gain, long-term loss scenario. After Pilate hands the obviously-innocent Jesus over to death to satisfy the crowd, he seems to have made the right choice. The riotous people are calmed and life goes on. But only four short years later, another crisis arises near Mount Gerizim, where a showdown between Romans troops and Samaritans leads to his being removed from office.

***The Good News for Achievers*** is that God's acceptance of us is based on something more firm than the popularity of our next decision. Our worth is held unchanged by the One who created us and is secured by the innocent Jesus, who suffered but triumphed over all fear and shame.

When your heart is filled with awe and overwhelmed by this good news, there will be no more room left to ask the question, "What are people going to do to me or say about me today?" Rather, you can say with the Psalmist, "The Lord is on my side; I will not fear. What can man do to me?"[4]

### → Pray

Father, You are big and man is small. Fearing You is the beginning of knowledge. Forgive me for the ways I allow others to control my life. Fill me by your Holy Spirit with the love of Christ so I live for You alone. I will rejoice in Your loving protection today.

4 Ps. 118:6

# Day 24 Reflections

**How has the fear of man been a major theme in your past?**

**How will remembering the gospel, this good news, enable you to do and say the right thing no matter the cost?**

## → Respond

Make it a goal to tell someone "no" today or to speak up for yourself.

## *Day 25:*

# Intimacy Problems

*Draw near to God, and he will draw near to you.*

—James 4:8

---

YOU CAN LEARN A LOT ABOUT THE closeness of your relationships by studying what you give them access too. Who do not let past your front door? Who makes it to your dinner table? What about the doors with the messes behind them?

Much like our homes, the intimacy of relationships can be measured by the access we offer: How much of our heart do they see? What doors to our thoughts, feelings, values, and motivations have been unlocked and which are we still guarding? How much of the mess is actually known to those we claim to love?

> I value intimacy, but on my terms—in small doses and when I am not in the middle of doing something.
>
> —Anonymous Achiever[1]

While Achievers generally have good relational skills and make great first impressions, intimacy doesn't come easy. True relational closeness has been described as "into-me-see," but as Riso and Hudson

1 Stabile, *The Path Between Us*, 105-106.

point out, this access is often not given even to our closest relationships: "From the outside, their marriage may look perfect, yet to their spouse real intimacy and emotional connection are missing. [Achievers] typically want the image of a successful relationship rather than the substance of a real one."[2]

Because of this, others may experience Achievers as emotionally distant or shallow—keeping conversation to safe topics like work—or even rude when social time is abruptly cut short. Others will often walk away feeling like they know their high functioning friends, but don't really know them.

God wants to know you even when you are distant, withdrawn, and guarded.

What if God feels the same way as your friends and loved ones? What if we've actually kept some of ourselves back from our Creator, too? The tragedy of not giving God the access He desires is that we are actually hiding from ourselves. In truth, we hide nothing from the God who "knit us together in our mother's womb," but the attempt to do so alienates us from the depths of our own souls.

Have you let your outward friendliness, natural charisma, or acts of service substitute for real connection? Remember, intimacy is not a matter of happenstance; it requires intentionality, which is not cultivated through detached observation but years of empathetic and vulnerable exchanges of the heart. Right now, you are as close to God and the people in your life as you want to be. It's a choice. The biblical writer James says that if you draw near to God, He will draw near to you;[3] intimacy requires mutuality.

***The Good News for Achievers*** is that God wants to know you even when you are distant, withdrawn, and guarded. He knows you have a busy heart and distracted mind, but calls you to Him still. He knows why you resist being vulnerable and yet invites you to embrace the openness to Him—to yourself—for which He made you. You can let Him and others in because there's nothing left to fear. Remember, Jesus said that greater intimacy with Him is now up to you: He stands at the door knocking because He wants to come in. But you must first unlock the door.

---

2 Riso and Hudson, *The Wisdom*, Kindle Locations 4204-4205.

3 James 4:8

## → Pray

Father, before I was formed in my mother's womb You knew me. I am able to know You because You are the author of my life. Thank You for creating me not just to serve You, but be known by You. Fill me with Your Spirit to take risks in being more vulnerable. Help me to share outwardly with You and others the innermost parts of my heart.

# Day 25 Reflections

**What are you afraid to let others see?**

**How will becoming more vulnerable remind you that you are loved for who you are rather than what you do?**

## → Respond

Read Psalm 77 and observe how vulnerable and honest Asaph is with the Lord. After meditating on the Psalm, try offering a prayer to the Lord with the same level of honesty.

*Day 26:*

# Get Behind Me, Feelings!

*Jesus wept.*

—John 11:35

How do you feel about feelings? Although Achievers can have a big heart toward those they work with, efficiency and performance are still the highest values, so they will "turn down the volume" on their emotions, tune them out, or put them in a box in order to keep moving. Thus, fully-engaging in their or others' emotions can be unfamiliar territory for fast-paced achievers.

Each type has methods of coping with life, and while most of these methods can help a person survive and even thrive, they often serve to block potential growth into becoming holistic people. For example, the ability of Achievers to read the feelings and needs of those around them appears to be almost supernatural, but what can occur is a disconnection from their own hearts and lived experience. Mirroring others' emotions back to them may help you seem empathetic, but it's usually just a way of hiding yourself.

> Feelings are like speed bumps—they just slow me down.
>
> —Wisdom of the Enneagram[1]

1 Riso and Hudson, *The Widsom*, Kindle Locations 4105-4106.

Ian Cron explains that "Threes do feelings more than have feelings. Because they can't access or recognize their feelings very well, Threes will unconsciously observe how other people are expressing their emotions and copy them."[2] But eventually those closest to you will figure out the game and may come to experience you as superficial or emotionally shallow—you may get the reputation of being personable but not personal.

In "Why Your Emotions Are a Good Thing," Carolyn Mahaney and Nicole Whitacre share what's at stake when we cut emotions from our lives:

Jesus was a kaleidoscope of emotions.

> "Even difficult emotions reflect reality and can move us to a better place. Feelings mirror the pain and suffering in our lives. Imagine losing a close friend or a beloved family member and feeling no grief or loss. What if you hurt someone you love but felt no remorse or shame? Imagine getting fired or failing a test and feeling no disappointment. It might sound nice to do without these painful feelings, but none of us can deny that emotions give meaning and depth to our lives."[3]

Jesus was a kaleidoscope of emotions, able to express the entire spectrum of human warmth and love, anger and frustration, grief and loss. When we say that Jesus was "fully human," we mean that He experienced it all—only more-so. His deep connection with the heart of the Creator gave Him deep insight to the human condition. He felt deep compassion toward the sick and infirm, anger toward evil and hypocrisy, grief over death and loneliness, and distress over humanity's waywardness.

Again, Achievers are very good at mirroring these emotions, but often fail to truly step into and live them as Jesus did. When we value efficiency and progress over emotion and depth, we turn the world into a flat black-and-white canvas, but God intended it to be in 3-D color.

---

2 Cron and Stabile, *The Road*, 136.

3 Carolyn Mahaney and Nicole Mahaney Whitacre, "Why Your Emotions Are a Good Thing," Crossway, October 13, 2017, https://www.crossway.org/articles/why-your-emotions-are-a-good-thing/.

***The Good News for Achievers*** is that our emotions are never far from us, if we will let them in. Take time to speak with those you love and trust: a spouse, partner, longtime friend, or even find a therapist or counselor. Express your desire to become more open and authentic to your true life experience; acknowledge that you can often mirror and be personable without being personal. Ask them to call you out when this seems to happen, and trust these people you love with everything swirling around in the heart given to you by the good Creator.

### → Pray

Father, there is no end to Your beauty and depth. You created the church in your image to reveal the many facets of Your glory to a lost world. Forgive me for substituting practical action for feelings. Thank You for sending Jesus to redeem me from stuffing and faking my emotions so that the Imago Dei might be restored in me. By your Spirit, make me fully alive.

# Day 26 Reflections

**In what ways do feelings threaten you or your goals?**

**How might feelings hinder short-term productivity but help long-term success?**

## → Respond

Download the "Feelings Wheel" and identify what primary emotion you've been feeling lately and why.

## *Day 27:*

# Style over Substance

*Do not look on [Saul's] appearance or on the height of his stature, because I have rejected him. For the Lord sees not as man sees: man looks on the outward appearance, but the Lord looks on the heart.*

—1 Samuel 16:7

---

Being an Achiever can be dangerous to your health in our American culture. Some say if the United States was an Enneagram number, it would be a Three (Achiever): Our society is full of self-promoting, productive leaders. With an eye to the number of "likes," those who can get stuff done and look good doing it are hailed as "winners," "influencers," or even "self-made." Our culture has become shockingly content with proud leaders who have moral failures, display racial or class superiority, or even sacrifice family, friends, and their community to move ahead. Because there isn't a penalty for cutting corners in the areas of character and integrity, pursuing style over substance is a real temptation.

> You attract people by the qualities you display but you keep them by the qualities you possess.
>
> —Unknown

One of the Achiever's greatest temptations is toward pretension. One of the strongest biblical models for the pretentious leader—one who accomplished much and made it look easy—is the first king of Israel, Saul. His imposing physique, sharp mind, and natural leadership skills endear his king-hungry people to him for many years.

Until his pretensions keep him from seeking God's direction and observing His commands, and even from being able to acknowledge others' God-given gifts.

As he ages into his privilege, Saul increasingly seeks counsel from men and not God, trusts his generals and on one occasion, even asks a medium's advice. He also increasingly lacks obedience, prompting the prophet Samuel to remind him, "Behold, to obey is better than sacrifice."[1] Finally, he fails to acknowledge the rise of his young servant, David, ultimately fearing and hunting him.

We must not prioritize public performance over private devotion.

Saul's story shows us the danger of prioritizing public performance over private devotion, and Achievers are similarly bent toward pretension and appearances. As Pastor Garrett Kell puts it, "Glory thieves feel hurried out of the prayer closet because we value being before men more than before God."[2]

***The Good News for Achievers*** is the path toward spiritual bankruptcy can be avoided. When we are able to raise our eyes above our own pursuit for success, we can more easily see God in all people and things, enabling us to seek the achievement of our human community over-against our own. When we elevate others (especially at our own perceived expense), we remind our hearts that God is not concerned with how much we are doing, but how much we are growing.

---

1 1 Sam. 15:22

2 Garrett Kell, "Stop Photobombing Jesus," The Gospel Coalition, 2017, https://www.thegospelcoalition.org/article/stop-photobombing-jesus/.

### → Pray

Father, You predestined all people to be conformed to the image of Your Son, Jesus. But I've often sacrificed inward obedience for outward appearance. Thanks be to Jesus for giving Himself up for me and cleansing me from the inside out. He presented me to You in splendor, despite my moral flaws. And I am thankful for His righteousness which makes me fit for the Holy Spirit to dwell within me. Thank You for the Holy Spirit, too, who helps me bear spiritual fruit I could never produce on my own.

# Day 27 Reflections

**When do you feel "hurried out of the prayer closet?" Why? Explain.**

**Who in your life could you elevate today?**

## → Respond

Begin a spiritual discipline to grow your character but don't tell anyone about it.

*Day 28:*

# The Feedback Fugitive

*The ear that listens to life-giving reproof will dwell among the wise. Whoever ignores instruction despises himself, but he who listens to reproof gains intelligence.*

—Proverbs 15:31-32

---

WHAT'S YOUR FAVORITE FUGITIVE-SPY MOVIE? THERE IS an endless string of them, from Jason Bourne to James Bond, to the simply named *Fugitive*, the plot-line is always the same but somehow they never fail to disappoint: The good guy (who everyone thinks is a bad guy) has to go on the run to escape arrest or avoid persecution. Throughout the movie, the exceedingly smart and capable fugitive deploys a variety of jaw-dropping tactics to mislead the frustrated authorities who, despite unlimited manpower and resources, are constantly one step behind.

> Criticism, like rain, should be gentle enough to nourish a man's growth without destroying his roots.
>
> —Frank A. Clark

Ironically, this fictional storyline could be "based on a true story" if you consider the way Achievers seek to avoid being captured by negative feedback. Feedback can be an "F-word" for unhealthy Achievers who want to avoid having their self-esteem deflated.

Since it's much easier to give than to receive, Achievers can be short and abrupt with others when offering criticism. But when they detect criticism advancing on them, they immediately hide by offering excuses or go on the attack, firing critical shots to keep themselves from being flanked. Welcoming feedback is a real challenge because your work and achievements easily become an "extra limb" and any feedback can feel like a personal jab. Like a pin to a ballon is criticism to the inflated ego.

But what if you viewed it differently? What if feedback didn't lead to shame but to greater success? What if, rather than an interruption, it became a critical step toward becoming a better leader? Make no mistake: Your success tomorrow depends on how well you receive feedback today. The wisdom of Proverbs says that a fool "Runs from life-giving reproof, whereas the wise person has the humility to listen to it." Ignoring feedback will only short-change you and your potential.

Your success tomorrow depends on how well you receive feedback today.

Are you ready to make some changes? The path of humility will mean admitting that you still make mistakes and your intuition is not always right. Beatrice Chestnut explains that Achievers may "fail to hear people out because they already have a plan firmly in mind and don't want to change course just because someone else has other ideas."[1] However, listening to the criticism of your plans and actions will almost always lead to growth and success—now and in the future.

***The Good News for Achievers*** is that God already sees us clearly. No amount of hiding from feedback will obscure our failures from Him (or even from the humans around us). Whether those words of correction come in the harsh hail of attacks or the gentle rain of constructive feedback, we can choose to hear the words as enemies or as God-given gifts and opportunities for self-correction. The roots of your identity are in Christ—you won't be destroyed. With the gospel in

---

1 Chestnut, *The 9 Types*, 120-121.

view, you will be able to invert the "fugitive" plot line and welcome those with feedback as the heroes in your life rather than the villains.

### → Pray

Father, thank You for making Your glory known by sending Your Son, Jesus, to dwell among us, full of grace and truth. If I claim to be perfect with no need of feedback, the truth is not in me. Remind me today that Your discipline toward Your children is a sign of Your love. Because I'm in You, I don't have to fear being shamed because my status is secure.

# Day 28 Reflections

**How do you avoid or defend yourself from feedback?**

**How can you communicate a receiving posture so others don't have to walk on eggshells around you?**

## → Respond

Practice receiving feedback by asking someday today, "How can I improve?"

## *Day 29:*

# Friends With Benefits

*But Jesus called them to him and said, "You know that the rulers of the Gentiles lord it over them, and their great ones exercise authority over them. It shall not be so among you. But whoever would be great among you must be your servant, and whoever would be first among you must be your slave, even as the Son of Man came not to be served but to serve, and to give his life as a ransom for many."*

—Matthew 20:25-28

---

WHO AMONG YOUR MANY COLLEAGUES, ACQUAINTANCES, AND family could you consider "close friends"? The truth is that Achievers seem to struggle more than other types with maintaining close friendships. The list of those they would consider close is likely short, and upon further inspection may mostly be made of "friends with benefits." In other words, these are people who offer some tangible return rather than the mere joy of

> What most people need to learn in life is how to love people and use things instead of using people and loving things.
>
> –Unknown

their presence, where the line between empowering and exploiting can easily (even if accidentally) be crossed. This is why, as Helen Palmer says, "Threes can let personal friends disappear, while work friends stay."[1]

Our value is not in our utility, but our identity.

Disempowering and exploiting friends can take many forms. If a friendship takes place in a work environment (particularly if you, as the Achiever, are in a position of leadership), you can easily load down your friends/co-workers with tasks, knowing they will be too afraid to complain and possibly damage a friendship and their work prospects. Alternately, people can be disempowered and exploited not by being given too much, but too little. For instance, you refuse to delegate or adequately train because you can do the job quickly and with quality—plus you won't have to deal with the trouble of navigating a relationship. Achievers can also hoard authority and responsibility from others out of fear of their potential and talents.

Do you value people for who they are or how useful they are?

***The Good News for Achievers*** is that our value is not in our utility, but our identity. Jesus reminded us that the very best Achievers are servants. They take the time to listen, experience and show authentic empathy, give up the spotlight, and hand over control. Servant leaders who focus on their own and others' identities work to make the group successful rather than just themselves, remembering that the best success is the fruit grown on others' trees. They seek to benefit their friends rather than the other way around.

---

1 Palmer, *The Enneagram,* 98.

### → Pray

Father, thank You for bestowing power and strength to me through the Holy Spirit—power that can be used to raise up others. Forgive me for using friends to gain power and "achieve" rather than using power to help others gain. Give me the mindset of Christ in all my relationships so that I might become a true servant.

# Day 29 Reflections

**As you look back, which people have made significant investments in your life? How were you empowered by them specifically?**

**How can you show greater love and loyalty to others apart from their functional use?**

**What can you do to expand your definition of personal success to include the success of the group?**

## → Respond

Ask someone, "What can I do today to make your job easier?"

## *Day 30:*

# Bent But Not Broken

*And Moses lifted up his hand and struck the rock with his staff twice, and water came out abundantly, and the congregation drank, and their livestock. And the Lord said to Moses and Aaron, "Because you did not believe in me, to uphold me as holy in the eyes of the people of Israel, therefore you shall not bring this assembly into the land that I have given them."*

—Numbers 20:11-12

---

WHAT ARE YOUR MOST COMMON STRESS TRIGGERS? Have you ever reached a breaking point that led to a total shutdown or even a public meltdown? Don Riso explains that Achievers often find themselves bent to the breaking point because they are "constantly working at a variety of projects in order to get ahead and make a favorable impression. This frequently leads them into situations in which they are uncomfortable or into work that they do not necessarily want to do."[1] It's precisely because the Achiever is so good at what they do that they may

> God tests us with stress before he trusts us with success.
>
> —Rick Warren

1 Don Riso and Russ Hudson, *Personality Types: Using the Enneagram for Self-Discovery* (HMH Books, 1996), 125.

rise to a level or role where they feel incompetent, inadequate, or not qualified to have.

Since Achievers often find themselves in places of leadership, the accompanying stressors often lead to their shutdown or meltdown: triggers such as inefficient meetings, personal or team failure or lack of productivity, not receiving credit for accomplishments, being blamed for the poor work of others, or being on the receiving end of too many negative emotions.

> Jesus was struck at the cross but reverberated compassion.

When they shut down, Achievers become disengaged and complacent. As Ian Cron explains, "They retreat to the couch with the remote or lose themselves in unproductive busywork. Seemingly worn out, they lose their characteristic optimism and confidence and become self-doubtful."[2] When they melt down, they display what is known as "Three Hostility," becoming "Directly hostile in a wide variety of ways, from arrogantly distancing themselves, to snide humor at others' expense, to sarcastic putdowns, to sabotaging and betraying people."[3]

Moses displays both sides of this breaking point throughout his long ministry. More than once, he seems to throw up his hands, telling God he would rather die than deal with the Israelites another moment. While the shutdowns often occur in private, his meltdowns occur in a much more public environment. For example, he strikes the rock at Meribah, disobeying God's order and seemingly taking credit for the miracle.[4]

Moses has a very stressful job—in the hot desert no less! It's certainly understandable that he bends past the breaking point at times. He listens to constant complaining, bickering, and backsliding; his leadership and authority are under constant threat by his own friends and family. We hear often of his self-doubt, frustration, loneliness, and anger. His final public failure at Meribah is the stated reason why he is denied entry to the promised land. Nonetheless,

2 Cron and Stabile, *The Road*, 145.

3 Riso and Hudson, *Personality Types*, 99-100.

4 cf. Num. 20:10-13.

Moses always recovers and stands with his people, leading them to the doorstep of Canaan.

***The Good News for Achievers*** is there is a way to bend without breaking. With proper mental health and trusted relationships who have your permission to call you out before you break down, you can establish safeguards and boundaries. From the safe distance of hindsight, you will be able to realize that your suffering—your lack of control—leads to transformation.[5] Let your stress lead to sanctification—a cleansing. Like Jesus was struck at the cross but reverberated compassion, your suffering and stress can lead you to experience grace in the midst of failure. This will allow you to have more loyalty, empathy, and compassion toward all.

### → Pray

Father, You initiated a plan to reconcile me while I was still Your enemy. Rather than being a god of wrath, You are the God who takes in the pain and suffering of the world and pours forth loving acceptance. Fill me with Your Holy Spirit to respond with forgiveness and compassion in the midst of stress and suffering like You did.

5 Richard Rohr, "Transforming Our Pain," Center for Action and Contemplation, February 26, 2016, http://cac.org/transforming-our-pain-2016-02-26/.

# Day 30 Reflections

**What most often triggers your stress?**

**Do you most often respond to stress and suffering by shutting down or melting down?**

## → Respond

Because others may be able to see the warning signs before you do, ask someone how they can tell when you are stressed out.

## *Day 31:*

# Too Busy To Parent

*Hear, O Israel: The Lord our God, the Lord is one. You shall love the Lord your God with all your heart and with all your soul and with all your might. And these words that I command you today shall be on your heart. You shall teach them diligently to your children, and shall talk of them when you sit in your house, and when you walk by the way, and when you lie down, and when you rise.*

—Deuteronomy 6:4-7

---

Whether you are a parent (or want to be a parent someday) or not, it's important to be aware that creating quality time for loved ones does not come easily for the average Achiever. Do you often feel too busy for your children or extended family like nieces and nephews?

> To be in your children's memories tomorrow, you have to be in their lives today.
>
> –Barbara Johnson

Seeing through a child's eyes could very well turn our perspective upside down.

Charles Francis Adams, the 19th century political figure and diplomat kept a diary. One day he entered: "Went fishing with my son today—a day wasted." His son, Brook Adams, on that same day, made this entry: "Went fishing with my father—the most wonderful day of my life!"[1]

> God is our perfect father whose love never ceases toward us.

Achievers have the ability to become great parents or mentors, but their constant pursuit of success can often get in the way. Jacqui Pollock explains that Achieving parents are friendly, upbeat, resilient, resourceful, and confident. But they also may set unrealistically high expectations, neglect the family, or lack energy when they are overly-focused on their work; they may become impatient or judgmental when children do things their own, inefficient way.[2]

Looking to Scripture for an example, we find King David thriving as a spiritual leader but struggling as a father. Amnom, Absalom, Adonijah, and Solomon go on to worship idols, gather a harem of lovers, and do unspeakable things. Job, on the other hand, is more present and involved with his children. He invents annual family feasts as a way to draw the family together. Additionally, Job wakes up early in the morning and offers sacrifices for his children "just in case" they had sinned against God in their hearts. His children are on the top of his priority list.

Like Job, do you see that spending time with children and teaching them to love God with their heart, soul, and might *is* God's definition of success? Children are a heritage and reward from the Lord!

***The Good News for Achievers*** is that though we are imperfect parents, aunts and uncles, or mentors, God is our perfect Father whose love never ceases toward us. He is never too busy and never fails to extend the hand of loving acceptance to His children. Just as Jesus received children with open arms, so must we. As you prioritize investing in children, remember to share your failures and frustrations,

---

1 Silas Shotwell, "Wasted Day," Bible.org, 1987, https://bible.org/illustration/wasted-day.

2 Jacqui Pollock, Margaret Loftus, and Tracy Tressider, *Knowing Me Knowing Them: Understand Your Parenting Personality by Discovering the Enneagram,* Kindle edition (Tracy Tresidder, Margaret Loftus, Jacqui Pollock, 2014), 76–77.

your doubts and questions; and above all, love them for who they are over what they do.

## → Pray

Father, help me to cling to the promise that if I train children up in the way they should go they will not depart from it when they get old. Fill me with Your Holy Spirit so that the children around me will see the gospel of Your love in action in their own lives. Let my greatest achievement be loving and accepting others just as You have loved me.

# Day 31 Reflections

**What work and technology boundaries can you create to protect quality time with your loved ones?**

**How often do you confess your sins and failures to children? How can you help them experience God's grace when they fail?**

**What opportunities are there in your home, extended family, or church community to teach and model the gospel for children or teens?**

## → Respond

If you are a parent, schedule a consistent weekly "date" with each of your children and let them pick the place and activity. If you aren't a parent, look for an opportunity to come alongside a family this week and offer your support!

# *Day 32:*

# Sailing with the Spirit

*The wind blows where it wishes, and you hear its sound, but you do not know where it comes from or where it goes. So it is with everyone who is born of the Spirit.*

—John 3:8

---

LIVING IN A CULTURE THAT INCREASINGLY ENCOURAGES us to spend more time doing than being has led to a "sloth in real self-development":[1] an almost atrophying of the spiritual muscles required to search ourselves and discern whether we have become the sort of people we want to be. Richard Rohr points out that Achievers are like bodybuilders who over-work one aspect of their physique (whatever part makes them look the best) to the detriment of other parts. In our entrepreneurial culture, heart work has fallen by the wayside, replaced by the drive to succeed.

> Spiritual formation is the idea that we must do something to enable God to do something.
>
> —Dallas Willard

However, when real heart-level work does become a priority, Achievers can go

---

1 Riso and Hudson, *The Wisdom*, Kindle Locations 4085-4088.

too far in the other direction by trying to do it all in their power. The process of becoming transformed becomes yet another task to achieve. While much can be accomplished through our own efforts, our self-development ultimately cannot. The Apostle Paul says things like we "are being transformed… for this comes from the Lord who is the Spirit,"[2] or we "walk by the Spirit," or are "led by the Spirit."[3] While the self-awareness offered by tools like the Enneagram can outline our path toward becoming, they are not sufficient to enact the change within. We need an external, transcendent power source.

> The process of sanctification is more like sailing than rowing.

Think about it this way: The process of sanctification (of living into the gift of God's adoption through Christ) is more like sailing than rowing. In a rowboat, you must do all the work: you must discern which direction to go and apply the right amount of force to get yourself there. It's exhausting work if you have far to go. But in a sailboat, the wind is the driving force. But sailing is not a passive activity; you must do the work of setting the sails and holding the ropes as the wind blows into them. The receptor of God's power must be prepared. In essence, sailing is an activity that requires participation from both the sailor and the Spirit (the Greek word for "wind," *pneuma*, is the same used for spirit). Together, making use of your tools and the freely-given wind, you can go distances that wouldn't have been possible in your little rowboat.

The Spirit is always blowing. Are your sails up or are you still rowing? As an Achiever, use your strengths of planning and goal-setting to properly set your heart's sails by integrating spiritual disciplines into your life such as meditation and prayer, solitude, fasting, study, service, confession, seeking counsel, and celebration. But remember that for you, the harder part will always be learning how to yield to the Spirit—the Helper—and even more difficult, waiting on His timing.

***The Good News for Achievers*** is that you can put the oars down. Take comfort that you can use your gifts to do the work, learn the disciplines, and use the tools,

---

2 2 Corinthians 3:18

3 Galatians 5:16; Romans 8:14

but you ultimately get to wait to be carried along by the Holy Spirit. The unasked-for and unforeseen grace offered through Jesus Christ is the same grace that is sanctifying you, as Paul reminds one of his favorite churches: "He who began a good work in you will carry it on to completion until the day of Christ Jesus."[4]

### → Pray

Father, it is You who works in me, both to will and to work for Your good pleasure. Thank You for causing me to be reborn not by my will, but through a miracle of the Spirit. You did not send Your Spirit to create a more improved self, but to make me a new creation. I am already Yours and there is nothing that can be done to separate us, so give me eyes to see Your transforming power at work within me and others.

4 Philippians 1:6

# Day 32 Reflections

**To what extent has your achieving orientation resulted in a "slothfulness in self-development"?**

**What about yielding control of your life to the Spirit terrifies you? Relieves you?**

**What can you do to integrate the spiritual disciplines from today's devotion into your current schedule?**

## → Respond

Find a book on spiritual disciplines and add it to your reading list.

*Day 33:*

# Rehab for Success Addicts

*Now you are the body of Christ and individually members of it.*

—1 Corinthians 12:27

> If I had never joined a church till I had found one that was perfect, I should never have joined one at all; and the moment I did join it, if I had found one, I should have spoiled it, for it would not have been a perfect church after I had become a member of it.
>
> –Charles Spurgeon[1]

THERE'S A PLACE WHERE YOU CAN GO to shine. It has a stage to stand on, a website to be promoted on and social media account that's waiting to post about you. It has a team of people in need of leading and a long list of roles that would make your resume look even better. This place is… the local church.

The church can easily become a "playground of admiration" for Achievers due to the constant need of help and the many front-and-center roles available. In today's church

1 Charles Spurgeon, "2234. The Best Donation," Answers in Genesis, 2017, https://answersingenesis.org/education/spurgeon-sermons/2234-the-best-donation/.

climate, the temptation and opportunity to expand our own footprint among the faithful is greater than ever thanks to enormous congregations and the various ways the Internet signal-boosts volunteers' work.

But would you be okay with being in a church that isn't attractive or cool? Would you be content if God called you to a church where the attendance hasn't grown in years or is even declining? What if the help it actually needs takes place behind closed doors and your involvement would not contribute to your success?

The Apostle Paul teaches that the church (both locally and globally) is made up of interdependent parts much like our physical bodies. If any one of these parts stop the flow by only taking, or begin to see themselves as preeminent, the entire body will become compromised, malnourished, and vulnerable. On the contrary, if the different parts figure out how to positively impact one another, the entire body will mature and grow strong together.

> The local church is not just the hope of the world, but your only hope.

Achievers can faithfully connect to the body of Christ by resisting the urge to use the community by serving others who could never thank you or pay you back. You can look for opportunities to serve on volunteer teams where you aren't the leader or center of attention, but are instead in a position to listen, learn, and support others. As Paul pointed out, "The parts of the body that seem to be weaker are indispensable, and on those parts of the body that we think less honorable we bestow the greater honor..."[2]

Lastly and perhaps most importantly, becoming a vital member of the body is to be deeply persuaded—as discussed in the previous devotion—that you can't achieve your way to spiritual growth. You desperately need a community of vulnerable relationships with whom you can share your strengths and successes, but more importantly, your weaknesses and failures.

The local church is not just the hope of the world, but your only hope. The church is a rehab community for the success-addict. You need a small gathering of those

---

2 1 Cor. 12:22-23

also on the path to becoming; a place where it's safe to take off the mask and show your authentic self. A group that will love you for who you are, not what you do. A group that will catch you when you fail—where it's safe to confess sin and not hide in shame. People who can encourage you to rest in the gospel after all the striving and achieving is done.

***The Good News for Achievers*** is that though our success has often left us short-sighted and self-reliant with an inflated sense of self-importance, Christ's path offers a new way into a new life. Through the interdependent body of those who gather in His name and seek to walk in His steps, we can be rehabilitated of our individualism and success addiction. Though no church is perfect, as Spurgeon says, it's "the dearest place on earth" for those who wish to be made perfect as the Father is perfect.

### → Pray

Father, You are my Lord, I have no good thing apart from You. Thank You Jesus for coming as our Savior, giving Yourself up for us so we may be one as You and the Father are one. Help me to sacrificially equip the church through the spiritual gifts You've imparted to me and humbly allow me to receive nourishment in return.

# Day 33 Reflections

**When have you chosen to serve in a recognizable role when your gifts would also help work behind the scenes? Would you choose differently in the future?**

**What gifts has God given you that would help the local church and other Kingdom-minded organizations?**

**How does Christ's loyalty toward an imperfect you motivate you to become more faithful to an imperfect church?**

## → Respond

Find a spiritual mentor who can help you walk faithfully with the Lord and assist you in discerning what He is saying and doing in your life.

## *Day 34:*

# Productive Prayer

*And when you pray, you must not be like the hypocrites. For they love to stand and pray in the synagogues and at the street corners, that they may be seen by others. Truly, I say to you, they have received their reward.*

—Matthew 6:5

ACHIEVERS CAN EXCEL IN BUILDING UP THEIR prayer lives if they put their minds to it. With a natural ability to focus and plan, and an innate optimism and confidence, they find it easy to schedule regular prayer times and lift up hope-filled prayers. However, life-changing prayer will almost always be one of the greatest challenges for the hurried Achiever. While it can be easy to set aside time to talk to God, it is much more difficult to block space to sit and just *be*. Prayer is beyond asking for things (even good things for others); in the end, prayer not primarily something you do, but something you get to participate in.

> This is the heart of prayer—not getting things from God, but getting God.
>
> —David Mathis[1]

Matthew chapter 6 says Jesus' primary issue with both the Pharisees' and Gentiles' prayer

1 David Mathis, *Habits of Grace* (Crossway, 2016).

practices is their desire to be seen as pious. To be seen as humble and heard as holy. But Jesus counters by asking what happens when no one is watching. With what spiritual posture, words, and silence do these same "holy men" approach God when no one can see?

God's desire for prayer is not that we post our devotional times on social media, feel accomplished by crossing it off the to-do list, or use it as a means to impress Him. Rather, prayer is simply a vulnerable encounter with God; a two-way conversation where you open your heart for God to share Himself with you and where you share your true self.

> Prayer is not primarily something you do, but something you get to participate in.

Real, honest prayers (especially for Achievers) tend to arise from a period of suffering, loss, or failure. When Achievers go through a personal or work crisis, they often become more committed to their close relationships rather than distancing themselves.[2] In success, Achievers can set themselves apart, but when your idols fail, you will return back to what's most important.

Valerie Woerner outlines tips for Achievers who are looking to cultivate a deeper prayer life.[3] It's important not to get discouraged by "unanswered" prayers. The "answers" to our petitions often come when we finally stop talking and bend our ear to the still, small voice waiting for us to be quiet enough to hear. To take the next right step while we wait faithfully for another to be illuminated is prayerful obedience. We also need to learn to verbalize our feelings and open up completely to God as the psalmists did. If God is the creator and sustainer of this world and ourselves, He can take our anger, grief, and disappointment. Practice replacing your well-worded requests with raw emotion (e.g. Psalm 77). Lastly, learn to embrace slow, still, and seemingly "unproductive" times. Silence and stillness can be very difficult for an Achiever, but it's the only way to allow the anxiety under the hood to surface—and it's a reminder that God longs to have us sit at His feet and just be.

---

2 Palmer, *The Enneagram*, 94.

3 Valerie Woerner, "The Enneagram & Prayer," Val Marie Paper, June 25, 2019, http://www.valmariepaper.com/the-enneagram-prayer/.

Additional practical steps could include: walking, working out, or doing something with your body so that your mind can focus; talking with God while you tidy up the house or do the dishes; using your leadership gift to initiate a prayer group to help yourself and others create more encounters with God; or trying the traditional fixed-hour prayer discipline where you intentionally interrupt your busy day to spend time with God in the morning, at noon, and in evening.[4]

***The Good News for Achievers*** is that God's presence and power that created and sustains all wishes to meet with you, and all you have to do is show up. The difficult work of quieting our busy minds and distracted hearts is no easier today than it was 2,000 years ago, but it is the place where the peace of our Father can be known—where His kingdom can come in our lives as it is in heaven.

### → Pray

Father, I admit that I want to look good to You and others even when I pray. Help me to be quick to pour out my heart and admit my sin. Thank You for sending Your Son, Jesus, to the cross to cover my shame so I can be completely honest and vulnerable with You when we speak. Open my ears to hear You knocking on my door daily so that I might open it and enjoy Your presence.

4 See Phyllis Tickle's *The Divine Hours* for a modern take on this ancient practice.

# Day 34 Reflections

**What if you didn't measure the success of your prayer life by "how often" or "how many words" but by how vulnerable you are?**

**What's at stake if you rush off today without an encounter with God?**

**Where can you create time to talk with God today?**

## → Respond

Start a habit of talking to God right after you wake up in the morning and right before you go to bed—when you aren't in "busy mode" and your feelings and anxiety are more accessible to you.

## *Day 35:*

# The Discipline of Celebration

*"Bless the LORD, O my soul,*
*and all that is within me,*
*bless his holy name!*
*Bless the LORD, O my soul,*
*and forget not all his benefits,*
*who forgives all your iniquity,*
*who heals all your diseases,*
*who redeems your life from the pit,*
*who crowns you with steadfast love and mercy,*
*who satisfies you with good*
*so that your youth is renewed like the eagle's."*

—Psalm 103:1-5

---

PRAISE AND RECOGNITION IS THE PREFERRED FUEL for an Achiever, but the joy that comes from celebration is the longer-lasting fuel. When you accomplish something great, do you stop to acknowledge it or do you immediately move on to the next challenge? When something beautiful occurs in your or loved ones' lives, do you stop to take it in? When was the last time you created space in your busy schedule to celebrate past wins?

We live in a "thank you, next" culture, but when the discipline of celebration is neglected, we are training ourselves to believe that what we've done or experienced isn't important or worthwhile—the only thing that matters it the next success high. This failure to pause and reflect on the beauty and positive success creates a cycle of feeling like we are never enough and so must rush on to the next win.[2] However, when your spirit is alive with gratitude, you will become a life-giver to your family and workplace.

The failure to reflect on positive success creates a cycle of feeling like we are never enough.

We are prone to forgetfulness. As Moses commands the people of Israel over and over, "Only take care, and keep your soul diligently, lest you forget the things that your eyes have seen, and lest they depart from your heart all the days of your life. Make them known to your children and your children's children."[3] If we do not actively plan and participate in moments of celebration and remembrance, we will not only become short-sighted, but we will also miss out on the beauty we have experienced.

In Scripture, celebration was planned and intentional. After the children of God are saved from the hand of Pharaoh and travel miraculously through the Red Sea, Miriam the prophetess picks up a tambourine and leads the women in a celebration dance. To celebrate the dedication of the wall of Jerusalem, the Israelites recruited two choirs and rounded up the best musicians for a big party. Celebration was even written into their calendar! Ancient Israel was required to gather three times every year to celebrate

> The decision to set the mind on the higher things of life is an act of the will. That is why celebration is a discipline.
>
> —Richard Foster[1]

1 Foster, *Celebration of Discipline*, 195.

2 Palmer, *The Enneagram*, 98.

3 Deut. 4:9

God and His mighty acts through festival holidays. The traditional church has followed Israel's lead, with a calendar marking seasons and days of expectancy, celebration, and penance.

Like the people of Israel set up stones to commemorate their entrance to the promised land and set up days to return to the monument and remember, how will you lay your stones of remembrance? How will you create more space to celebrate both the past beauty and the new?

***The Good News for Achievers*** is that many of the practices we have already discussed are easily adapted to the task of celebration and remembrance. Write about it in your journal and take time on retreats to remember. Gather with your community to feasting, sing, and dance. Begin your conversations with the question: "Where have we seen God working?"

### → Pray

Father, I bless Your holy name! You have forgiven my sins and redeemed my life from the pit. Your Son, Jesus, received a crown of thorns so that I would be crowned with Your steadfast love and mercy. By Your Holy Spirit, help me to never forget all You've done for me. Enable me to lead a celebratory life that rejoices in You always.

# Day 35 Reflections

**What are you celebrating?**

**How can you devote more time to the discipline of celebration?**

**How can you spend more time, personally or in meetings, calling out greatness in others?**

## → Respond

Start a new tradition or rhythm of celebration and stick to it.

*Day 36:*

# Dropping the Poker Face

*For if anyone thinks he is something, when he is nothing, he deceives himself.*

—Galatians 6:3

---

EXPERIENCED POKER PLAYERS ARE ALWAYS QUICK TO explain that winning requires something more than playing a good hand well. World-class players are not only masters of knowing the odds related to their hand, but also their opponents'. While great players can guess which cards the people across the table are likely to have, champions know by becoming expert readers of expression and body language. More than that, they must be able to hide their own emotions to keep the other players guessing.

> The only lies for which we are truly punished are those we tell ourselves.
>
> –V. S. Naipaul[1]

While a strong "poker face" may help you win competitions, it can become a handicap to authentic personal growth. Ian Cron points out that "Threes can mask and postpone feelings so they won't blow their 'I have it all together' cover. In the moment, they can be feeling

1 Beatrice Chestnut, *The Complete Enneagram: 27 Paths to Greater Self-Knowledge* (Berkeley, CA: She Writes Press, 2013), 311.

depressed, angry or scared and maintain their upbeat, confident poker face."[2] Achievers are great at faking-it-till-you-make-it because deep down they believe they won't be loved unless they look like they have it all together.

The cardinal vice of an Achiever is said to be deceit, but before they can mislead those across the table, they will first deceive themselves.[3] As the Apostle Paul says, "For if anyone thinks he is something, when he is nothing, he deceives himself."[4] We lie to ourselves by identifying with the successful persona we work so hard to create, then turn around and present that version of ourselves to the world.

Therefore, the path of growth for an Achiever often begins by moving toward greater authenticity—first with ourselves, and then with the face we show the world. Riso and Hudson explain, "Authenticity means manifesting who you are in the moment. When Threes are present, they are simple and able to speak the truth that comes directly from their hearts. At first glance, this may not seem like much of an achievement, but if we think about it, we realize how rarely we present ourselves to others in this way."[5]

> Jesus loved us when we didn't have it all together.

Dropping the poker face involves being honest with yourself about who you really are, what your true desires are, and what you are feeling in the moment. It also means refraining from concealing your opinions or emotional distress from others, so don't withhold your true self for fear of what others will think. After all, they aren't your opponents in the game of life, but your fellow-travelers. And you must notice when you are "turning it on" and becoming someone else, someone you wish you were, or believe others wish you were.

Be fearlessly authentic. Drop the cards and the mask you use to hide them. Pretending you have it all together all the time sends the message to others that the only person you need to depend on is yourself; that it's possible to pull ourselves up by our bootstraps and succeed apart from grace. However, the Apostle Paul

---

2 Cron and Stabile, *The Road*, 136.

3 Riso and Hudson, *The Wisdom*, Kindle Locations 4076-4077.

4 Gal. 6:3

5 Riso and Hudson, *The Wisdom*, Kindle Locations 4397-4399.

is refreshingly transparent, almost reveling in his weakness and exalting Christ's strength. He tells his Corinthian church plant, "I was with you in weakness and in fear and much trembling" and admits to his protégé Timothy that he is the "chief of all sinners."[6]

***The Good News for Achievers*** is Jesus accepted and loved us when we didn't have it all together and couldn't pull ourselves together. Follow the Apostle's example: reveal and revel in the weaknesses that allow others to bring their full selves to you. Authenticity breeds authenticity, as Dr. Julianna Slattery wrote: "Realize that the story of how your brokenness has caused you to depend on Christ is much more powerful than any other story you could tell to try to impress people."[7]

### → Pray

Father, Your grace is sufficient for me, for Your power is made perfect in my weakness. Help me Holy Spirit to be transparent and show that the all-surpassing power in my life is from You alone.

---

6 1 Cor. 2:3; 1 Tim. 1:15

7 Julianna Slattery, "Take Your Masks Off: The Value of Authenticity," Crosswalk.com, 2009, https://www.crosswalk.com/faith/women/take-your-masks-off-the-value-of-authenticity-11559579.html.

# Day 36 Reflections

**How does wearing a poker face distort the message of the gospel to others?**

**What's the best and worst thing that could happen to you if yourevealed your true emotions and desires?**

**Where can you be more authentic this week to encourage authenticity in others?**

## → Respond

Instead of nodding along in a conversation today, take off the mask and share how you really feel even if your true emotions might hurt your image.

## *Day 37:*

# Bending the Truth

*You are of your father the devil, and your will is to do your father's desires. He was a murderer from the beginning, and does not stand in the truth, because there is no truth in him. When he lies, he speaks out of his own character, for he is a liar and the father of lies.*

—John 8:44

---

DO YOU EVER SHARE HALF-TRUTHS TO PROTECT yourself from shame, embarrassment, or failure? Bending the truth is a common struggle for Achievers: like an experienced tailor, they will custom-fit the elements of a story to suit their own needs. One of the most public examples of this in recent memory that had international reverberations is the scandal leading to President Bill Clinton's impeachment in 1998.

> A half-truth does more mischief than a whole lie.
>
> –Ivan Panin

All of America was pulled into the President's affair with the young staffer Monica Lewinski when her private conversations with a co-worker were recorded and publicized. Once confronted, Clinton refuted the allegations and famously said, "I did not have sexual relations with that woman, Miss Lewinsky": a half-truth tailored to conceal the nature of their relationship and control as much of the damage as possible. But once physical evidence found its way to a grand jury, the President was forced to admit he did have "inappropriate intimate physical contact" with Lewinsky. The sordid affair tarnished the legacy of a president and broke the lives of those caught in the cross-fire.

While very few of us have the ability to create unrest like this, Clinton's story is instructive for unhealthy Achievers; it shows how their desire to constantly present themselves as put-together and successful impacts their lives and every person near them. Achievers may tell people what they want to hear (or what may hurt the least) rather than giving them the hard truth. They may confess more acceptable sins to give the appearance of authenticity but hide the bigger ones to protect themselves from experiencing shame. They may feel in the moment that a half-lie is a necessarily evil to protect themselves from unwanted shame.

The pain they experience from your deceit is greater than the pain you would have received from admitting your failure in the first place.

But in the end, when the truth comes out, this "harmless" act ultimately harms someone else. The pain they experience from your deceit is greater than the pain you would have received from admitting your failure in the first place. It's much easier to forgive a failure than a deceiver.

The path of growth for Achievers is to pursue a ruthless honesty that refuses to gloss over the big and little lies for themselves and others. It involves a commitment to confess sin, admit mistakes, and "tell the whole truth and nothing but the truth." It means no longer airbrushing personal or work failures or inflating successes, but letting them be what they are.

***The Good News for Achievers*** is though we continually break the commandment to not deceive our neighbor with whole lies and half-truths, if we confess our sin to God, He is faithful and just to forgive us and cleanse us of all our deceit. We can first begin to tell ourselves the truth, to say aloud (even if no one is there to hear at first) what we fear to acknowledge. We can have the difficult conversations with those who are most intimately impacted by our words and deeds and begin the process of healing. Though the path is rough, we owe it to ourselves, our loved ones and community, and ultimately to the God who already sees us as we are.

### → Pray

Father, Your character and promises are trustworthy. It is impossible for You to lie. You sent your Son Jesus to be the way, the truth, and the life. Thank You for sanctifying me in truth. Help me to not walk in the footsteps of the father of lies today, but rather to walk in Your footsteps—following the "Father of lights, with whom there is no variation or shadow" (Jas. 1:17).

# Day 37 Reflections

**In what situations do you find yourself bending the truth the most?**

**What are you trying to either protect or prevent when you bend the truth?**

**Why do you think it's sometimes difficult for you to tell the whole truth?**

## → Respond

Talk to someone who hasn't heard the "whole truth" from you yet.

*Day 38:*

# Hope to the Hopeless

*May the God of hope fill you with all joy and peace in believing, so that by the power of the Holy Spirit you may abound in hope.*

—Romans 15:13

---

ACHIEVERS TYPICALLY WAKE UP TO A GLASS is "half full" view of life. These eternal optimists offer hope to an often hopeless world through their tireless pursuit of and belief in their dreams. Their "can do" attitude drives all around them to begin hoping. As Riso and Hudson explain, "They embody the best in a culture, and others are able to see their hopes and dreams mirrored in them."[1]

> There are no hopeless situations; there are only people who have grown hopeless about them.
>
> –Clare Boothe Luce

In this world, there is plenty of hype and cynicism, but hope is more difficult to come by. Hype is just exaggerated optimism, a distracting placebo. Cynicism, is the opposite of hype—it's the natural response to disappointed hope. Rather than distracting us, cynicism throws up walls of defense around the heart to keep us from feeling the sting of disappointment.

1 Riso and Hudson, *The Widsom*, Kindle Locations 3802-3803.

But real hope does not distract or wall-off—it faces up to life as it is, then cries out with a defiant "nevertheless." "Hope is not a lottery ticket you can sit on the sofa and clutch," says Rebecca Solnit, "it is an axe you break down doors with in an emergency."[2]

Christian hope is unique due to its source. The anchor of the hopeful Christian life lies in the resurrection of Christ, in the miraculous renewal of this dust-to-dust life; it is hope in the midst of hopelessness, a light in the midst of darkness. It is the epitome of that defiant "nevertheless," which leads us to affirm life and renewal when all around us seems to fall into death and decay. As David Bentley Hart says,

Rather than putting hope in your own achieving efforts root it in the resurrection.

> Easter is an act of "rebellion" against all false necessity and all illegitimate or misused authority, all cruelty and heartless chance. It liberates us from servitude to and terror before the "elements": It emancipates us from fate. It overcomes the "world": Easter should make rebels of us all.[3]

***The Good News for Achievers*** is that God has called you for such a time as this to be a dealer of hope to the down-and-out. Though even the most optimistic Achiever cannot always be hopeful, you have a deep reserve that could renew the lives of those around you. Rather than putting hope in your own achieving efforts root it in the resurrection. Rather than hoarding hope for yourself, steward it daily as a part of your ministry to strengthen those who feel defeated.

---

2 Rebecca Solnit, *Hope in the Dark* (Haymarket Books, 2016), 4.

3 David Bentley Hart, *The Doors of the Sea: Where Was God in the Tsunami?* (Wm. B. Eerdmans Publishing, 2005).

### → Pray

Father, while we were unable to call heaven home, You sent Your Son, Jesus, to save us through His work. You have filled us with the Holy Spirit who makes us abound in hope. Help us comprehend the hope we have and the power of the resurrection so that we might help others find joy and peace.

# Day 38 Reflections

**How does Jesus' resurrection speak to every hopeless situation?**

**How can you respond better to others' pessimism?**

**What are some ways you can encourage people who are cynical or just hyped up, but live with no real hope?**

## → Respond

Contact someone who is in a hopeless situation right now and use your gift of faith to inspire hope.

*Day 39:*

# Blind Spots in Love

*Love is patient and kind; love does not envy or boast; it is not arrogant or rude. It does not insist on its own way; it is not irritable or resentful; it does not rejoice at wrongdoing, but rejoices with the truth. Love bears all things, believes all things, hopes all things, endures all things.*

—1 Corinthians 13:4-7

---

Performers become more tentative and afraid when they enter a secure relationship. Their strength lies in leadership, where the placement of attention favors tasks over feelings.

–Helen Palmer[1]

THE FIRST TIME WE SIT BEHIND THE wheel of a car, we discover that what we can't see may hurt us. That's why we can't afford to ignore our blind spots and be aware of the flow of traffic and the ever-changing rhythms of the road. The same is true when navigating relationships: our failure to see the needs of those with whom we live and work can lead to unintentional pain.

---

1 Palmer, *The Enneagram*, 92.

The Apostle Paul gives us a detailed list of potential blind spots in his beautiful chapter on love, 1 Corinthians 13. First on the list? Love is patient—perhaps the greatest challenge and blindness plaguing Achievers. When others want to talk about their problems or simply engage in unhurried conversations, it can be difficult to turn off the desire to move on, refusing to believe that if you stop "life will lap you."

Achievers must also learn to let go of control. Are you always the driver in your relationships or do you ever take the passenger seat? Do you allow others to direct the conversation and it's pace—even if the resulting discussion doesn't lead to something getting accomplished? When decisions need to be made, are you an incorrigible backseat driver, offering comments and betraying your frustration or impatience in your body language?

Love is patient—perhaps the greatest challenge and blindness plaguing Achievers.

Achievers tend to avoid conversations relating darker thoughts and emotions. Your natural optimism will often lead you to tune out negativity or pessimism, sometimes causing you to become dismissive or abruptly change the conversation.[2] When exposed to others' suffering or sadness, the stressed-out you may be tempted to cut others short and say, "Ok, let's do something about this now."[3] But remember, your job is not to shut out the darkness, but to transform it into resurrection hope for those who cannot see beyond their own pain.

Achievers often drop relationships when they get difficult, depressing, or if someone more desirable comes along. When you check your blind spots, do you see an inclination to change your circle of friends with every new season of life?[4] The path of growth for Achievers will always include cultivating abiding, loyal relationships that don't have any professional benefit, but rather exist solely to support those involved.

2 Ibid, 95.

3 Ibid, 96.

4 Riso and Hudson, *Personality Types,* 120-121.

***The Good News for Achievers*** is that God first loved us even when we weren't loyal to Him in return. He sent His Son, Jesus Christ, to reveal and save us from our blind spots in love. Through Jesus, the multi-faceted love of the Triune Godhead has been made visible to us. Just as a diverse spectrum of bright colors shine through a crystal prism, so too does the patience, kindness, truth, and enduring love of the Father shine through the Son with magnificent glory. If you have seen and tasted this radiant love, you ought to go and love others in the same way today.

### → Pray

Father, You are love itself. When it comes to pursuing intimacy with You and others, my love falls incredibly short. Forgive me for not paying attention to the blind spots that keep me from loving others well. Enable me by Your Holy Spirit to demonstrate a kind, patient, and unrelenting love from the well of Your steadfast love which endures forever.

# Day 39 Reflections

**How has God showed you patience, kindness, and steadfast love through all your ups and downs?**

**Which aspect of Paul's definition of love do you struggle with the most?**

**Because our blind spots come into view quickly in our most secure relationships, what do you need to change to be more receptive to those who can see the person behind the mask?**

## → Respond

Invite someone to have an unhurried conversation with you during the day and follow through on it.

## *Day 40:*

# I Think I Can

*I can do all things through him who strengthens me.*

—Philippians 4:13

---

DID YOU EVER READ THE CHILDREN'S STORY, *The Little Engine That Could*? Surprisingly, *The Little Engine* was actually a sermon illustration before it became one of the greatest children's stories of all time. In the early 1900's, boatloads of immigrants from Europe sailed into New York Harbor seeking the American Dream. Dr. Joseph Cramer suggests that these immigrants, living in slums and working in dark and often dangerous factories, would have been the perfect recipients for Reverend Charles S. Wing's illustration on hope, hard work, and self-discipline. "The Story of the Engine That Thought It Could" went on to be published in the *New-York Tribune* on April 8, 1906.[1]

> God never calls us to any kingdom responsibility we are capable of pulling off on our own.
>
> –Jon Bloom

The engine's continual chorus of "I think I can!" perfectly describes the Achiever's working superpower, speaking to an innate

1 Joseph Cramer, "Joseph Cramer, M.D.: The Little Engine That Could Choose," Deseret News, July 1, 2013, https://www.deseret.com/2013/7/1/20521885/joseph-cramer-m-d-the-little-engine-that-could-133-choose.

drivenness that gets results and helps the team go further faster. Being the "lead engine" that pulls others along with them is their preferred role, which is why they often become the poster child of their profession. They are the model of team recruitment and motivation, goal setting, and rooting out the system's inefficiencies.

Achievers are great at "feeling out" the expectations of whatever group or organization they are a part of, like the Apostle Paul claims he has "become all things to all people."[2] They know how to meet the unique needs and goals of all people, are competent, resourceful, and efficient. Their knack for multi-tasking helps their seemingly inexhaustible engine climb the hill faster. If you're looking for the Achievers in your midst, they'll likely be the ones eating lunch in their car or reading on the treadmill—because every second counts.[3]

When they get going, Achievers are a force of nature. As Helen Palmer explains, "The typical American Three does business like a football quarterback. You try every trick in the book to keep the ball moving in the right direction... Once in motion, Threes get tunnel vision and tune out the opposition."[4] But a truly successful quarterback must bring the whole team along, or their individual effort won't translate to team victories. While you could get up the hill faster than everyone else, true success is how many people you bring up with you. As one African Proverb said, "If you want to go fast, go alone. If you want to go far, go together." You were not given a tremendous leadership gift to show off or become the star, but to carry others up with you.

While you could get up the hill faster than everyone else, true success is how many people you bring up with you.

***The Good News for Achievers*** is that you can do all things through Christ who strengthens you. When problematic people, challenging circumstances, or seemingly impossible tasks "get hitched" to you and you start to get tired, slow down, and tell yourself "I don't think I can," you must remember that the power

2 1 Cor. 9:22

3 Palmer, *The Enneagram*, 91.

4 Ibid, 100.

is not within you. You can do all things through Christ. Great spiritual reserves of hope have been given to you to ascend the hill of servant leadership and take part in Christ's ongoing work of renewing the world.

### → Pray

Father, I am not able to ascend the hill of the Lord because I do not have clean hands or a pure heart. But thanks be to Jesus Christ for saving me on the hill of Calvary. Though I work hard, I am not the one who makes myself better; it's Your Spirit-empowered grace at work within me. Help me to remember today that nothing is impossible with You.

# Day 40 Reflections

**When have you noticed your "can do attitude" in full effect?**

**Why is it more tempting to climb the hill of success alone? Why might it be more fulfilling to take others with you?**

## → Respond

Think about all your goals and dreams. Start working toward something today that seems impossible without divine intervention.

## *Prayer for Achievers*

FATHER, I AM DEEPLY GRATEFUL TO YOU for creating me in Your image as Your child. You created me to specifically reflect Your undying hope and power to succeed. I confess that I've lived for others' approval rather than for Your glory. Ignoring my need for rest, I have often worked too much and viewed others as obstacles instead of precious souls You created and love. But You, being rich in mercy, sent Your Son Jesus to die on a cross for my flawed self, not my accomplished self, and forever exchanged my failures for His successes. Christ alone achieved my salvation—and whatever I accomplish in this life will be cast down at Your feet in the life to come. Putting off my old mask of deceit and putting on my new self that is clothed in Christ, I will seek to live as a human being rather than a human doing, embracing feelings and failures, prioritizing people over projects, and reminding myself that love always trumps tasks. Amen.

# *Next Steps*

I'm so proud of you for finishing this 40-day journey. Knowing that you are an over-achiever, I'm guessing it took you less than 40 days. Am I right? You're probably wondering: *What now? My eyes have been opened, I've grown in greater self-awareness and empathy, and now I'm ready to take the next step!* Here are some ideas:

1. If you haven't yet, put your trust in Jesus. You can do this in your own words or by repeating the Prayer for Achievers on the previous page.

2. Ask a friend, spouse, mentor, or discipler to meet regularly with you to discuss the insights God has revealed to you through this book. Invite them, along with your small group, to get a devotional on their type and share what they learn with you.

3. Join a church community where you can continue to grow in your knowledge of God and self. Like we mentioned, it is the perfect rehab for success addicts.

4. Follow "Gospel For Enneagram" on Instagram, Facebook, or Twitter to continue learning and engaging.

5. Visit our website, gospelforenneagram.com, to find more helpful links and resources.

6. Email me with any thoughts, questions, or feedback to tyler@gospelforenneagram.com. I'd love to hear from you!

**Download my free resource called "Should Christians Use The Enneagram?" at gospelforenneagram.com.**

# *Acknowledgements*

My wife: Lindsey, you show me the gospel every day by loving me for who I am and not what I do. Thank you for your tremendous encouragement to be a writer and for bearing with my workaholic tendencies. I want to be more like you.

My editors: Joshua Casey, thank you for bringing your incredible creativity to the table. Your re-rewrites helped elevate my writing to a whole new level. Stephanie Cross, having your attention to detail and passion for both the gospel and this project gave me tremendous confidence.

My coach: John Fooshee, thank you for your Enneagram coaching and partnership. I'm deeply grateful for your willingness to come alongside me and put wind in my sails.

My influences: I wouldn't have been able to pull this off without a multitude of direct and indirect influences such as pastors, teachers, and writers (including you, mom!) over the years. I'm deeply grateful for the spiritual heroes that have come before me and shaped me.

**www.GospelForEnneagram.com**

**Follow us:**

 /GospelForEnneagram

 @GospelForEnneagram

 @GospelForGram

Made in the USA
Monee, IL
24 August 2023

41584155R00105